FALCONRY
— FOR —
BEGINNERS

FALCONRY
FOR
BEGINNERS

Lee William Harris

SWAN HILL
PRESS

First published in the UK in 1998
by Swan Hill Press, an imprint of
Quiller Publishing Ltd

Reprinted 2000, 2002 and 2006 (with amendments)

British Library Cataloguing-in-Publication Data
A catalogue record for this book
is available from the British Library

ISBN 1 85310 893 6
    978 1 85310 893 8

Printed in Hong Kong

Swan Hill Press
an imprint of Quiller Publishing Ltd
Wykey House, Wykey, Shrewsbury SY4 1JA, England
Tel: 01939 261616 Fax: 01939 261606
E-mail: info@quillerbooks.com
Website: www.countrybooksdirect.com

Dedication

This book is wholly dedicated to my son,
David Lee Harris,
whom I love more than words could ever say.

Acknowledgements

A book of this kind would not be possible without the help and enthusiasm of close friends and colleagues. Therefore I should like to express my gratitude to Jim Moss of Crown Falconry, PC Paul Beecroft for the section regarding the law, Philip Stapleburg for the section on Dealing with Common Illnesses and Ailments in Birds of Prey, Neil Gwilt of Reflections Photography, Jane Stephens for the drawings and illustrations, and Geoffrey Hobbs for his invaluable time spent reading the manuscript. I especially thank Alan and Belinda Hicks from the Sky Falconry Centre for all their help.

Finally I should like to thank my parents for their support and encouragement throughout the writing of this book.

Foreword

How lucky we falconers are. Not only do we spend a great deal of time in the company of beautiful birds, we also have the added stimulation of the ultimate working relationship.

As a youngster I always had a passion and esteem for birds of prey. What struck me most of all when I studied pictures of hawks, owls and falcons was their eyes. To this day, when I peer deep into the eyes of a raptor I see power and pride. But as a young boy I did not realise that the practice of falconry existed. I was simply aware of certain owl and raptor species and read book after book on them in their natural environment.

Around the age of ten, however, a trip to the local library provided my first encounter with the mind-boggling world of falconry. The book I borrowed catapulted my life into a new dimension, for I then realised that bird and man could work together as a formidable team. As more books became available, I read them, and read them again, spellbound.

My interest in falconry remained consistent, even after I left school. The natural progression was to find and attend a course, which I achieved after weeks of searching. The course built on my basic knowledge, but I thought that owning a bird of my own was almost certainly out of the question. Yet the one thing I wanted more than anything else was to be a falconer and have the chance of training and flying my own hawk. As the months passed, my impatience became unbearable. The desire to fly raptors overwhelmed me, the burning ambition still ate away deep within.

Then quite by chance I attended a game fair. In a far corner stood a large marquee. Birds of prey graced the inner covers, sitting proud upon their perches waiting to be flown. The display team that day was quite superb, flying a fantastic array of birds. I sat mesmerised, my desire to be a falconer growing stronger and stronger. Afterwards, I gingerly approached the man in charge, who was extremely helpful. We had a long chat that left me in high spirits, believing there were ways in which I could become a part of this extraordinary sport.

Not long afterwards, and after starting full-time employment, I managed to acquire my first bird, a common buzzard. At last I could put my knowledge into practice. I flew the buzzard every day until it reached peak fitness. Unfortunately, as with the vast majority of buzzards, its ability to chase and kill quarry was, to say the least, pretty dismal. However, it did have courage and a heart full of enthusiasm, and working with it taught me the basics of training and entering a bird of prey.

Having spent a season with the buzzard I felt it was time to move on. I chose a Harris hawk as my next bird, and quickly realised that it had everything I required, plus a little more. The Harris had speed, temperament and compatibility, but most of all it had the ability to catch quarry. Throughout this period, I built further upon my knowledge of falconry terminology and developed such skills as coping, imping and leathercraft. The learning process was fully underway.

Shortly after receiving the Harris hawk, I found myself enticed into the world of longwings. I invested in a saker falcon, a large, powerful bird that had a genuine hunger to fly game. Flying longwings posed a new challenge. On reflection I should have waited a little longer, at least another season or two before I became involved with, and tried to understand the technicalities of, hunting falcons. The training methods I adopted were somewhat different from those of the broadwings, and to be perfectly honest, I did not do the bird justice. Although I flew hard every day I was a little in the dark as to exactly what I was doing and, more importantly, what I was seeking to achieve. Consequently I decided to part company with the saker after only the first season and concentrate mainly on broadwings, shortwings and owls.

These days I am lucky enough to be able to dedicate my life to the sport I love. It is one of the very few things in life for which I have total admiration, commitment and respect. The massive challenge of training a bird of prey, getting the most from its God-given natural ability, will always excite me. All too often the 'downs' outweigh the 'ups' – the death or theft of a bird is something I still find very hard to accept – but it is a question of persevering. Falconry brings together man and bird, and with this comes the ultimate desire and determination to be successful.

I hope that you have as much pleasure reading this book as I have had in writing and researching it. Above all, however, I hope it will give would-be falconers something to think about before pursuing the ancient sport of kings.

Finally, for obvious reasons, the prices quoted for equipment etc. can only be approximate.

Contents

CHAPTER ONE

Introduction to Falconry

The History of Falconry

The word 'raptor' comes from the Latin word meaning 'to seize'. It is quite appropriate, as raptors spend a great deal of time chasing and seizing other animals. Raptors are no different from lions and tigers; all are predators and all are competing to survive. Equally, predators keep the natural world in some kind of even balance. If they did not exist the environment would soon be overrun with other species battling for food, which would inevitably be in short supply. In the wild, raptors prefer to kill either the old, the young or the sick, as they present the easiest food. In this way the healthiest and strongest always survive to breed and maintain their own population.

Birds of prey are pure hunting machines, and they are delightfully equipped to kill. The vast majority possess the accustomed hooked upper mandible, which is ideal for ripping apart the flesh of captured prey, and all have very powerful legs with the feet containing sharp, deadly talons, with which they hold down and kill their quarry. There are around 290 species of raptor throughout the world, and they can be divided into various groups: vultures, harriers, kites, hawks, buzzards, eagles, ospreys and falcons. There are also over 160 species of owl.

Falconry, which is said to be the oldest sport in the world, is the training of birds of prey to chase and kill wild quarry for the falconer. It is probable that the first ever falconer trapped a young raptor in the hope that with the bird's natural skills it might be tamed and trained to catch wild quarry as a means of putting fresh food onto the table. It is of Oriental origin, having started in China as early as 2000 BC. In such countries as Persia, Japan, India and other Asian countries it developed in about 600 BC. It quickly moved into Egypt and is the subject of some of the oldest Egyptian wall paintings. The sport was introduced into Europe by the Romans, and came to England in the second half of the ninth century AD. Alexander the Great practised falconry, as did Alfred the Great and Ethelbert II, the Saxon King of Kent. Mary Queen of Scots was a keen falconer and flew a merlin, *Falco columbarius*, from horseback – the merlin was classed as a lady's bird.

Shortly after the Norman conquest of 1066, falconry became particularly popular in England. Many people from all walks of life kept birds of prey, but the longwings were mainly reserved for nobility. Indeed, at that time the species of raptor one carried marked one's station in society. A king would carry a gyr falcon, *Falco rusticolus*, a fresh longwing introduced into England around 1066, an earl would carry a peregrine falcon, *Falco peregrinus*, a yeoman a goshawk, *Accipitor gentilis*, a priest a sparrowhawk, *Accipitor nisus*, and a servant a kestrel, *Falco tinnunculus*. The knights of the Middle Ages were permitted to fly saker falcons, *Falco cherrug*, a large powerful longwing and another favourite of kings. A squire would carry a lanner falcon, *Falco biarmicus*, a persistent hunter of quail. A young squire would be allowed a hobby, *Falco subbuteo*.

During this period trained hawks and falcons were very valuable, and in many cases they were used for paying ransoms, fines and rent. In fact, falconry was taken so seriously, and birds were so highly prized, that the penalties for stealing a bird were extremely severe. During the reign of Edward III, the theft of a trained bird was punished by death. A law passed by Henry VII decreed that anyone caught stealing a bird from the nest on another person's property should be imprisoned for a year and a day. One of the most bizarre punishments was dictated by Burgundian law; the thief would have six ounces of flesh removed from his breast by the bird that he had stolen.

Falconry remained highly fashionable in England until the beginning of the seventeenth century, when enthusiasm began to decline. During the Restoration period, after 1660, it again revived a little, only to go out of fashion once again in the early part of the eighteenth century, when shooting birds on the wing became popular in Britain. During the eighteenth century, Holland was the capital of European falconry, with the biggest array of birds. Wild birds were trapped using nets during their migration. Dutch families passed the art of falconry from generation to generation.

In recent times falconry has again become popular. It is pursued in Britain and Latin America, and has enthusiasts spread widely across Europe, the United States and Canada. And in certain parts of West Africa, the Middle East and the Orient, it has never lost its popularity.

Throughout the world, birds of prey have been seen as a sign of power. In northern Borneo the hawk is believed to be a messenger of God, and is treated with great honour, its carved wooden image standing proud as it guards houses to ward off evil spirits. Tribes in the Amazon and in Ecuador make their arrows with the primary feathers taken from hawks, whilst other tribes smear their bodies with the juice gathered from boiled talons before setting out for a day's hunting. Some tribes pay homage to the sharp-shinned hawk, *Accipiter striatus*, for its keen eyesight. Medicine men in many tribes use the feathers of owls, eagles and hawks in their head-dress as a sign of status and power.

Little has changed in the practice of falconry over the centuries. It is a sport of tradition, and the traditional approaches and values are firmly fixed into the minds of today's falconers.

Getting into Falconry

For many years I have participated in a wonderful sport, or rather a way of life, that has given me tremendous personal joy and many hours of intense delight. No other sport can bring man closer to nature than falconry. Being in the company of such beautiful creatures, often amongst breathtaking scenery, gives me a feeling of total contentment.

To watch a raptor soaring high into the heavens, using the thermals to her own advantage, is something very few people will ever experience. The phenomenal co-ordination, balance and strength with which these birds are blessed are quite remarkable. A peregrine circling high over abundant moorland before stooping at well over 100 mph in an attempt to outmanoeuvre a grouse, the silent ghostly silhouette of a barn owl hunting low over a favourite hedgerow just as another frosty morning starts to bite – this is just a small part of the appeal of birds of prey, owls and falconry in general.

The intimacy between hawk and keeper is a most private and fragile relationship. It should be based on passion, understanding and respect. If one upsets the bird, forgiveness is a long time coming – if there is forgiveness at all. Falconry is probably the most demanding of all field sports, but if it is taught correctly and then pursued to the highest level of professionalism, it is in my opinion the most satisfying. The long, lonely hours of sitting and manning one's hawk, building upon her confidence are rewarded when at last she bends her head and accepts a mouthful of food presented to her upon a gloved hand. This, for me is an emotional moment, as her acceptance becomes apparent.

The taming and training of all birds of prey must be taken at the right pace, for if it is hurried the end result may be of an unacceptable standard. At the Eagle-Owl School of Falconry, students are told to learn the art of being patient. Highly strung, quick-tempered people will never make the grade. A young hawk requires hours of understanding, so patience is the order of the day.

About 50 per cent of the students who come to us do so because they have admired a bird of prey flying display either at a fête or game fair, and have fallen in love with a barn owl or been mesmerised by the sight of a falcon stooping at great height and speed to a padded leather lure. Whilst I think flying displays are an excellent way of educating the public to the whole concept surrounding falconry, I do not feel it is the best reason to become involved in the sport – although to some extent that is how I became hooked. The birds used for display work are extremely fit and in tip-top condition. The falconer will have put many hours of hard work and dedication into each one of them, thus making them a joy for all to admire. The novice therefore only sees the end result, birds to be proud of and not the endless time spent in getting them prepared.

Personally I am a big fan of flying displays, and when I am not working myself I enjoy visiting various venues and meeting old friends. To conduct a display is very exciting, and when everything comes together – perfect weather and a delightful performance from a favourite longwing – it without doubt gives a boost to the spirits. And whether or not that is the intention, displays will always tempt a minority to go off and try their hand at the sport. A few of these people – a small percentage – worry me, however. The sensible ones will locate a falconry club or better still attend a falconry course. But some will simply go to the library, read a book or two on falconry, buy a bird and think they are falconers. *If only it were that simple.* Over the years I have been alarmed at the way many beginners conduct themselves towards buying, keeping and caring for birds of prey. I can only put this down to a lack of knowledge, and the fact that many beginners just do not understand the basic rudiments associated with daily management and hawk ownership. Some, for example, even buy the hawk first before they have the living quarters and equipment.

This book has been put together to help the genuine beginner, as I appreciate just how difficult it can sometimes be to get started. It is intended to set you off in the right direction, explaining thoroughly the correct way to approach owning a bird of prey or an owl. At times you may feel that I am almost discouraging you from taking up the sport. I can assure you this is not the case – after all, the more people there are involved in the sport, the better. Providing we do our best at all times making sure to conduct ourselves in the correct manner, falconry can only grow stronger, thus safeguarding its future.

It is vitally important, however, that you realise the many complications involved. To earn the title of 'falconer', you will have to develop a vast array of skills – fieldcraft, leathercraft and basic butchery to mention just a few. You will have to understand food values and the measures to take should your bird become injured or show signs of illness whilst out in the field. You will need to study and recognise game, in order to give your bird every possible opportunity of making a kill. Falconry is not just about the size of the bag at the end of the day, but it is nice to make the occasional kill. You should study the ways of the rabbit, becoming familiar with its uncanny behaviour; rabbits are normally abundant, and they are the most often hawked quarry. You should think of using dogs and ferrets; they can influence the size and quality of your bag come the end of the hunting season.

The skills I have mentioned will take years to acquire, but acquire them you must. Listen to and watch falconers, and question what you do not understand. All falconers have their own individual ways of doing things; in time you will too. Those who get it right can enjoy season after season of good, solid, consistent hawking, whilst those who get it wrong will probably not last a season. Bad falconers will blame either their bird or the land they are flying over for an unproductive day, whilst good ones will blame only themselves. Beginners who start off and continue with the right attitude, determined to master the art, will become very capable and worthwhile participants who will enjoy the benefits of falconry to the full. Those who are not prepared to cultivate this attitude are strongly advised never to start.

In a way, it is sad that so many birds of prey are easily come by. I have seen barn owls for sale in pet shops and, even worse, being kept in glorified parrot cages. This is not the way to approach buying a bird of this kind. Birds offered for sale in this way have no dignity. There are many excellent breeders who are dedicated to the well-being of their birds, and you should only buy from them. No matter what any pet shop manager may tell you, birds of prey do not make pets. They are fliers, and fly extremely well – my birds look forward to their daily flight and I know that the freedom of being airborne gives them as much pleasure as I get from watching them. An overweight bird kept in an aviary and denied exercise will only become bored and unhappy.

To some extent falconers are born rather than taught, and developing the many skills and learning the techniques is a long and often lonely process. Having said that, most experienced falconers will make beginners welcome and do their best to guide them through the early learning stages, thus making the lonely road a little easier.

CHAPTER TWO

Getting Started

Thought is by far the most important word used in this book. If some beginners had put more thought into what they were doing, I am confident that they would have been successful sooner, and reached a much higher level of skill – or not pursued falconry at all. Too many people are under a misapprehension about what is needed to prepare a hawk for the field. They often believe that birds of prey fly to us purely out of love. When asked about flying and hunting-weights, their faces show only dismay. But successful hawking consists of many important elements, all of which have to be mastered.

Before buying a bird of prey you must first be aware of, and fully understand, the extensive commitment you will be taking on.

You must be sure that:

- you can devote endless time to the well-being of your bird
- you acquire a manageable bird that has been correctly reared
- you invest in a bird that has the potential to live up to your own expectations.

A buzzard cannot and will not achieve the same level of field success as the Harris hawk, so correct bird selection is vital.

No matter what species you select, all will require your devoted attention every day. Although raptors may give the impression of being strong and robust, it is my experience that if they do fall victim to illness they tend not to put up a great deal of fight. This is why it is imperative to spend time with your bird daily, checking for early signs of sickness. To open the aviary door and casually throw food in is cruel and shameful. It requires only a few minutes to take a bird up onto the fist and check her over, and you could be saving her from suffering. If you cannot find time to do this, then you will never find the time to train and maintain a bird of this kind. A hawk that is only flown once or twice a week will never reach full potential. She will certainly miss or decline kills that would have been taken had she been fit. Any hunting bird of prey will quickly become frustrated if it is constantly being outflown and outmanoeuvred by quarry. If you take your bird into the field you owe it to her to make sure she is in a healthy state so that she has every opportunity of achieving what comes naturally to her.

Before obtaining a bird of prey, you must first look at your lifestyle

A falconer manning his bird

and commitments. You must be truthful and ask yourself if you can afford not only the bird, but everything you will need. Taking up falconry is not cheap. The costs – of the bird, the equipment, the aviary and the food – will soon mount up, and you will be spending many hundreds of pounds. So before you start, you should be sure that falconry is something that you are prepared to stay with. If you realise that you have made a terrible mistake after you have started, you will lose around 50 per cent of your outlay.

It is relatively easy to buy a bird of prey today, but the commitments thereafter will become more onerous. As long as your bird lives, and this can be for many years, she will depend on you to attend to her every need.

There is no magic surrounding this sport; with time and dedication all birds can look good and be a pleasure to work with. I remember a very competent falconer once saying to me, 'There is no such thing as a lazy bird, but there are many lazy falconers.' Over the years I have often thought about that, and I am still not sure whether I totally agree with it, but it does contain some truth.

Obviously one has to work, but being in full-time employment should not put you off. I have friends who are very successful falconers whilst having to work extremely long hours. Their birds are always fit and keen, and enjoy many kills come hawking season. So you can have the best of both worlds; it is purely down to your professionalism and enthusiasm.

It is important that you invest in a bird that has been correctly reared. My advice to all beginners is buy an eyass, this being a young bird taken from the parents, of the year. This is not to say that the older birds you will see offered for sale within specialist magazines are problem birds, it simply means that you will have total control of its training. It is preferable to use a breeder who has a reputation for supplying healthy young, even if this means paying a little more. A big mistake that beginners often make is to buy a bird that lacks the natural ability to achieve the kind of field success that they envisage. Consider just what it is you expect from a bird, and make sure your final choice has the potential to live up to your expectations.

Having acquired your bird, in order to do yourself and it justice you will need to be totally dedicated and develop a vast in-depth knowledge of every aspect of falconry. It is not easy and will take a very long time to perfect. Never underestimate a bird of prey's mental capacity. They are shrewd, quick to learn and in my opinion reasonably intelligent. Complacency will simply hinder your progress and may end your hawking days prematurely. Put a lot of thought into every decision you make, and you will not go far wrong.

Five Important Questions

A newcomer to falconry is entering into a sport that is both physically demanding and mentally trying, fraught with many different aspects and unforeseeable dilemmas, all of which will try the falconer to the limit. It is therefore vital that before you invest in a bird of prey or an owl you become familiar with the obstacles and challenges, which are all too often disregarded or brushed aside. It is far better to sort out potential problems long before any commitment is made. Falconry is a sport that produces new surprises every day – this is one of the things that makes it so appealing. Nothing is guaranteed, nor should it be. Any sport that involves the partnership with an animal is a long-term undertaking. Your ability will be reflected throughout in your bird's progress.

There are five questions which you need to ask yourself before you start. Although they are basic, they all concern potential problems that should be firmly assessed. You must be honest and answer as realistically as you can. If you cannot answer some of the questions positively then think of possible solutions. For instance, you may have a regular outlet for hawk food, but as yet have been unsuccessful in locating suitable land. This is something you can get around, but you could have problems if you are away from home five days a week. So providing you can see a way of overcoming any problems, you should be able to go ahead.

The five questions are:

- How much time can you spend with a bird?
- Do you have access to land over which to fly and hunt your bird?
- Can you afford it?
- Can you get a regular supply of good-quality food?
- Are you often away from home?

How Much Time Can You Spend with Your Bird?
It probably goes without saying that the more time you spend in the company of your bird the better she will be. An eyass of the year freshly taken from her parents would have seen a human only briefly whilst being rung. She will be nervous and long to be back inside her aviary with her mother. She will have no reason to accept you, and consequently will do everything in her power to break free. With shortwings or broadwings I usually allow them two weeks of liberty, giving them a chance to get accustomed to their new environment. Throughout this period I will do no more than let them see me daily.

After the two weeks are over, the manning process begins. This basically involves getting the bird to accept you. I will spend around four hours a day, every day, just sitting with my bird, trying to steady her and win her trust. This is a slow process, as you are trying to achieve many things. You will require your bird to sit on the fist, readily accepting food when it is offered. She will need to overcome her fear of human companionship, and allow you to place your hands over any part of her torso without running the risk of being bitten or, even worse, footed. She will need to become accustomed to the many different noises in the world around her, such as cars, motorcycles, tractors, barking dogs and the general noise of towns. It is impossible to give a precise estimate of the time it will take to man a hawk, as it largely depends on your skill and the species of hawk you are working with, but up to two months is not uncommon.

Manning sessions should always be undertaken outdoors, and away from the things that the bird is familiar with. Never half-heartedly train a bird in or around its own living quarters. It will naturally achieve much more when it is in familiar surroundings, and then when it is in the middle of a wide-open field, it will become insecure and it will feel as though you are starting the manning process all over again.

If you do not put thought and commitment into every manning session, you will ultimately achieve nothing. And it is imperative that once you start the process you continue with it fully until the training is complete. There is no sense in spending weeks of intense manning only to let it lapse for a day or two; you run the risk of losing all that you have achieved.

Owls are different, as they will need to be imprinted by means of hand-rearing from around two weeks old. Hand-rearing brings many delights, but constantly cleaning up owl mess is not one of them. A two-week-old owl will need feeding around the clock. A responsible person must be with the bird at all times attending to her every need, which requires patience, commitment and time, but most importantly it requires knowledge.

For the first six weeks, the baby owl will not be able to get into too much trouble. Thereafter things will tend to become more fraught. She will soon begin to walk and flap around the house. Eventually she will start losing her fluffy down, which you will find in every crack and crevice of your home. By this time, she will be feeding of her own accord and you will begin to find pieces of rotting meat hidden in all manner of places. Even at this stage the bird will still need monitoring at all times.

If owls were not hand-reared, they would be aggressive and antisocial, allowing no one close. Training would be extremely difficult and you would run the risk of being badly injured. Even a barn owl can inflict nasty wounds.

For the first ten to twelve weeks of an owl's life, she should live indoors as part of the family. At ten weeks old, you may start to weather her, and finally at twelve weeks she may be tethered permanently to her perch within the aviary. Small to medium-sized owls do not need to be tethered inside their aviary once the training is complete, and even larger birds can enjoy the freedom of free flight if the weathering is large enough.

In summary, if you intend purchasing either a hawk or a buzzard as your introductory bird, you will need to find up to four hours each day for as long as eight weeks just to complete the manning process. This will be followed by daily training sessions of two to three hours for up to three weeks. On completion of the training, you will need to fly your bird hard every day to achieve and maintain fitness.

If you decide on an owl, you will have around ten weeks of hand-rearing before you start manning the bird to your local environment. This will involve daily sessions of up to three hours for two to three weeks. The training takes the same time as for hawks and buzzards, but I find that owls tend to lose their fitness much sooner.

The delights of falconry will only be achieved by those who are prepared to find the time and commitment for their bird.

*Do You Have Access to Land over which to Fly
and Hunt Your Bird?*

Good hawking land is vital to your bird's performance, but finding it could be one of the greatest problems that you will come up against. Very few people have the luxury of either owning suitable land themselves or knowing someone who does. It is very important, therefore, to sort out your hawking land before you purchase your bird, as you may find it harder than you first imagined.

Some people believe that they will be able to take their bird along to the local municipal park or council forest and train it there. I can only say that I have never come across anybody who has been granted permission to do this. Even if you received approval, there is one major problem that would immediately arise. People are fascinated with birds of prey and in no time at all you would have an audience around you, which would be extremely off-putting for your bird and slow the training process quite considerably. Privately owned land is a far better proposition. Not only will there be fewer people to pester you, there would be a lot less activity to overcome. Your bird will be much more at ease and take to the training process much more

Ideal hawking land

quickly. Moreover, as a beginner you can do without all the fuss and attention that you will inevitably receive from members of the public.

Adjacent to my house is a cemetery, which was, I thought, an ideal place to take a small bird to fly. In a far corner was a disused section of land, and I once walked a young barn owl there for some fresh air and a manning session. Never had I been so popular; my barn owl was soon a celebrity and relished all the attention he received. It finally got to the stage where people would actually ask when I would next be over. But when I eventually came to train the bird, it was impossible. There were crowds of people disrupting me and my bird was not progressing. Sadly I could no longer go there.

Having privacy to train your bird and get her flying fit is imperative, and it is well worth spending time to locate and acquire the right kind. And no matter where you live, you should be able to find some. In my experience, providing you ask politely, stressing the fact that you will respect their land, farmers are often quite happy for you to use their fields. But when approaching a farmer, you should make it perfectly clear that you may need to work dogs or ferrets and not take his approval for granted. Nor is it acceptable to think that you will be allowed to ask friends along for the day. A farmer is putting a great deal of trust in you when he gives you permission to fly his land, for he will not necessarily know that your intentions are completely honourable. So do not spoil your relationship through lack of courtesy.

The majority of farmers have problems with rabbits and will be only too pleased to have you work their land. Providing you are honest, trustworthy and straight with them right from the beginning you can eventually form a good relationship. Under no circumstances should you ever intentionally go onto land where you do not have permission. The only time this rule may be broken is if your bird chases quarry and ends up pitching or killing in another field. If this should happen, retrieve your bird as quickly as possible, apologising if you are asked what you are doing. My policy is to track down the landowner and apologise even if I have not been seen. This kind of courtesy may even extend your hawking ground.

When looking for land one of the key things to take into account is quietness. There should be no major roads bordering the area, and no shooting on or around it. And of course, a good supply of quarry is most welcome.

If you are really struggling to find adequate land, the best course of action is to locate and join a falconry club. The majority of clubs will have land available to them and I am sure you would be most welcome to attend field meets throughout the season with your bird.

I have attended many field meets with beginners who have sought out good land, but still struggle to find quarry for their bird.

Basically this is because they do not understand field management. A good falconry course will supply the relevant methods required to be successful. Understanding the countryside is a very complex subject, so learn the basics and educate yourself as you go along.

You will not be successful every time you go out. In some respects this is what makes falconry so challenging. Rabbits can move pretty fast and will waste no time at all in finding cover, almost before your bird has left the fist and got into first gear. Some slips are pointless and will give your bird no hope of a kill, which is where field management and experience comes into its own. The use of pointers and spaniels will make all the difference when searching for quarry, as will ferrets. As with your bird, you must also understand the ways in which these animals work. Some people keep working-ferrets in an appalling condition, which is just not acceptable. I believe a good ferret is just as important as my bird, so it deserves the same high quality of life. Falconry is all about teamwork. Good birds, dogs, ferrets and land all contribute to successful, worthwhile hawking.

Respect people's land as if it were your own. For example, if a ferret kills and stays underground and needs to be dug out, always replace the soil. And at Christmas it is a nice gesture to present your landowner with a bottle of whisky. This is a small price to pay to maintain a happy relationship. Remember, it is far easier to lose land than it is to acquire it, so look after and enjoy what it has to offer.

Can You Afford It?
The students we see at the Eagle-Owl School of Falconry have different ideas about the start-up costs of falconry. This is quite understandable, as some are on far higher incomes than others. It is therefore difficult to attain any true judgement from their opinions. My own view is that falconry can be a very expensive sport, especially if silly mistakes are made early on. We once had someone on a falconry course who had already purchased a barn owl. The bird had no living quarters and minimal equipment, as it had been bought on impulse. On the second day, he brought along some items of equipment to show my head falconer, who had the embarrassing job of telling him that what he had been sold was totally unsuitable for the bird. He had a bow perch that was bulky enough to accommodate a large female hawk; barn owls are far better suited to block perches. The leather anklets and jesses he wanted served onto the bird were incredibly thick, with no suppleness, and they were also far too large. He had been sold a chrome-plated swivel that would not only rust in time but again was far too bulky and heavy for a barn owl. The leash was so thick that my head falconer was unable to tie an adequate knot. The supplier obviously had no qualms about supplying unsuitable equipment to a vulnerable member of the public.

Start-up costs largely depend on the species of bird that you buy, the quality and amount of equipment you purchase, and the size of aviary you construct. Many beginners try to cut costs by making certain items of equipment themselves. From what I have seen, the end result is normally of a very poor standard and certainly not suitable to be used with a bird. Suppliers put a great deal of thought into the equipment they design, so you are well advised to buy your first batch from a reputable dealer.

Building your aviary should be the first step towards hawk ownership, but before you do this, or purchase any equipment, you must be absolutely sure about the bird you will eventually be purchasing. It is silly to buy equipment for a female European eagle-owl only to buy a male buzzard. The entire range will be useless. Mistakes like these can easily be avoided, providing you put some thought into every decision. If you do not, you will be in for some expensive surprises.

The correct order in which to do things when taking up falconry is:

1. Attend a reputable course.
2. Decide upon the bird best suited to your personal needs.
3. Build an adequate aviary.
4. Purchase *all* the necessary equipment.
5. Buy your bird. That should always be the last item on your list.

There are many equipment suppliers who will only be too pleased to guide and advise you on your specific needs. Prices vary quite considerably from one supplier to another, but then so does quality; I would advise anyone to send off for as many catalogues as possible. A list of suppliers can be found in either *Cage and Aviary Birds*, a weekly publication that is available from all leading newsagents, or the *Falconer's Magazine*, available every quarter by subscription, and compare prices. There will be a supplier to suit everyone's pocket. However, try not to get carried away by products that are ridiculously cheap. As with most manufacturing, cheapness is often associated with poor quality and unsuitable after-sales service.

If you decide to buy a Harris hawk, along with everything it requires, you will be looking at an initial investment of approximately £1,700. If you get a buzzard, it will be approximately £1,200. Obviously much depends on the breeder used, and the equipment supplier.

But start-up costs are just the first of many expenses. You will have constant food demands and probably also vets' fees. You should have your bird registered with a vet who is fully qualified and experienced with birds of prey. You can, if you wish, insure your bird against vet fees, and this is something I would certainly suggest looking into.

At some stage you will need to renew items of equipment and maintain and repair your aviary. If you plan to keep and work ferrets they too will require housing, feeding, maintenance and equipment, and once again vet fees are something to take into account. Obviously the same applies with a working dog.

Can You Get a Regular Supply of Good-quality Food?
Obtaining a regular supply of hawk food should not present too much of a problem; obtaining good-quality food at a realistic price may. There are many outlets that currently supply food suitable for birds of prey; once again *Cage and Aviary Birds* or the *Falconer's Magazine* should be a good starting point. You may be fortunate enough to live in an area where there are outlets supplying top-quality food. If you do, count yourself extremely lucky; the vast majority of people do not have this luxury and will have difficulty finding even one that is within reasonable travelling distance.

It is always preferable to use a supplier who is based near to where you live, so that you can pick up a fresh supply when you want. But make sure that they have a large variety of food which is always in stock, as you should be aiming to feed your bird a healthy mixed diet.

If you are unable to find a local supplier, or one close enough for you to collect food, then you may have to settle for a delivery order. This gives you the inconvenience of having to be there when it is delivered, and you will have to ensure that it is delivered on time, and not two or three days later than agreed, as this may put you in an awkward position. From what I am told, deliveries from food companies appear to have improved dramatically over the years. In fact, there are those who prefer to buy this way and are prepared to pay a little more for the service. So if you are happy with the reliability of a delivery then buy this way. I would suggest, however, that you learn the whereabouts of another outlet just in case.

If you are ever stranded for food, you will find that most good pet shops stock a minimal range, but the price is often double that in a specialist stockist, and the quality frequently poor. Whilst you should never try to save money when buying high-quality food, I do object strongly to paying too much, especially when the food is of an unacceptable standard. Unfortunately the owners of most pet shops do not fully understand the difference between good and poor food. In the course of time you will learn to judge the quality of food just by looking at it in its frozen state. The way it is packaged and the cleanness of the fur will eventually enable you to make a very good informed guess. Chicks for instance should have clean yellow fur with no patches of discolouring. It should be easy for you to pull one apart from another. If you need to hit them with a hammer, the chances are they will dry out wet and smelly.

If you join a falconry club, you will probably find that one or two members supply food. You will then have the comforting feeling of knowing it is of an acceptable standard and at a price that is fully justified.

Never refreeze meat, and make absolutely sure that chicks have been frozen down properly, thus eliminating the risk of salmonella poisoning, which will kill a bird. Even prompt veterinary treatment often has no effect. Buy your chicks already blast-frozen; they will be slightly on the dearer side, but you will have peace of mind.

Again, it is vitally important that you take adequate measures to locate a reliable food source long before buying your bird.

Are You Often Away from Home?

As I have said, the amount of time and commitment that is involved in owning and training a bird of prey is quite considerable. And it is important to understand that this means *your* time and commitment.

Many new falconers with jobs which often take them away from home believe that they can rely on a friend or neighbour to feed and maintain their birds. This is not the case, and no reputable experienced falconer will do it. To leave your bird in the hands of an untrained person is wrong. If it were to become tangled or straddle the perch, there would be no one to free it.

Moreover, you will want your bird to become familiar with you and accept you, as you will be the one working her in the field. To achieve this, you will need to spend time with her daily, focusing on her often irrational behaviour and trying to make sense of her inconsistent attitude. It is impossible to understand your bird if you are rarely around to monitor her character.

There are no short cuts, no easy ways. Everything is achieved through time and devotion, and if you cannot find time for your bird, then there is no point in pursuing falconry. The sport is all about bird and man working together and forming a competitive team, and a balance as delicate as this can only be achieved successfully by an in-depth understanding of and respect for your bird, which in turn will only come with total commitment and time in her presence.

So you should never acquire a bird of prey or owl if you know that you will regularly have to rely on someone else to care for it. Obviously there are going to be times when you will need the help of friends and family, but barring unforeseen emergencies, these periods should never extend beyond a day or so. Your bird is your responsibility; it is your duty to take care of her.

If you do have a job that often takes you away from home, or if you take three or four holidays a year, you should not take up falconry until your lifestyle changes. There are no 'boarding kennels' for birds of prey, and not many falconers would welcome the responsibility of looking after someone else's bird. Therefore, unless you can find a knowledgeable falconer who *is* prepared to take charge of your duties whilst you are away, you should not go.

I have heard many stories of people going away and leaving their bird with two weeks' supply of food. This is disgraceful behaviour and falconry can well do without that sort of person. In summer the food will go rotten and soon be alive with maggots, and in winter, you run the risk of food thawing during the day and then refreezing at night.

There are people who would love to see falconry banned. People who come into the sport and do not treat their birds with the respect they deserve give its opponents invaluable ammunition and could destroy the reputation and credibility of responsible participants. A genuine falconer would not dream of leaving a bird alone for a single day, let alone two weeks. I suspect that those who invest in a bird of prey when they know full well that they do not have the time to care for them do it to seek attention. But falconry is the oldest sport in the world, with a long history and tradition, and it was never intended for attention-seekers.

To summarise, therefore, it is better to wait until life offers you a greater degree of flexibility before going to the trouble and expense of starting a sport which you will not be able to pursue to the full. Falconry is available for all to enjoy, but if you will have to split yourself in half as it were in order to achieve anything worthwhile, then it will quickly become a burden.

Attending a Falconry Course

Any beginner who is serious about progressing should attend a well-structured course. Here you will receive a good understanding of the many aspects of falconry. Reading a book or two or watching a video is a very good initial step, and something I would fully recommend, as it will show you the level of commitment needed before you become too involved. But at a falconry course an experienced falconer will be present to answer your specific questions, which books and videos cannot do. You will also be shown precisely how to develop the necessary skills.

There have been many keen students who, after attending a course, have decided that the sport is not for them. If that is the case, the course will have fulfilled one of its functions in giving them an understanding of what is involved.

If you do decide to attend a course, then you need to ensure that you get value for your money and time. It is important to find a course that will give you the grounding that is best suited to your

A falconry class in progress

own particular needs. Many establishments now run falconry courses, and a list can be obtained from the *Falconer's Magazine* and *Cage and Aviary Birds*. Most are very helpful and strive to provide a good service. At the Eagle-Owl School of Falconry, for example, we constantly try to make the courses more constructive, and every student who comes to us is asked to tell us ways in which we can improve. Over the years this information has helped us enormously to develop our current syllabus.

Initially, you should gather a list of the schools and decide which would be most convenient for you; you should then send off for information, which should help you decide which course is best suited to you. You must take into account the following:

- **Structure**. Ask yourself whether the course covers the points you feel are most important. This is the most fundamental point to consider when choosing a school.
- **Time**. How many days does the course take, and do you think it is practical to learn what you need in that time?
- **Class size**. How many students are there on each course? Schools that admit a dozen or so will, I believe, struggle to assess each student's strengths and weaknesses.
- **Cost**. This should be a relatively minor consideration. If you believe that a particular course is right for you, but is dearer than another which is less suitable, then you should wait until you have sufficient funds to attend.

At the Eagle-Owl School of Falconry, we run three courses. We have an **introductory day** for those who have a love for birds of prey or owls, but do not want to be a part of the sport. It gives them a chance to get close to the birds, see how they are trained and learn a little about the history of the sport. Although limited, this course is also suitable for potential falconers, as it contains information about hawk ownership and management.

The **falconer's course** is designed for those who do want to be a part of the sport. It is held over a three-day period beginning on Friday morning and ending on Sunday evening. The programme covers bird selection, equipment, training, hunting, diet, basic health care, the law, understanding the countryside, lamping and working dogs and ferrets. Students make simple items of equipment which they can take away for their bird, if they buy one. Unlike the introductory day, we do not fly falcons or small to medium-sized owls on this course, as we do not believe they are suited to novices. After attending this course, we feel that students are in a position to own, train and maintain a bird of prey to an acceptable standard. As with all our courses, we offer a follow-up service which enables former students to contact us if they have any points which need clarifying.

The **longwing course** is for those who have been practising falconry for some time and want to move on to flying falcons. It is held over a two-day period and covers key issues such as bird selection, hybrids, training, lure swinging, working dogs and hunting.

All our courses are restricted to a maximum of five students and cover more or less the same ground as others. Some schools, however, believe their version of our falconer's course should be held over a five-day period, others two days. The important thing is to decide what you feel is right.

Some years ago beginners did not have the choice they have today. Equipment costs were high, falconry schools were scarce and birds were far less available. The falconry market is now much more competitive, however, which is a good thing for the falconer, as businesses can only survive by giving a good service at a reasonable price.

Weatherings

Aviaries, or weatherings as they are called in falconry, should be strong, robust and built to withstand frequent high winds. They should have three solid sides, with a full sloping roof leaning towards the front. The front should consist of a good-sized door to allow for easy access and the wire mesh should be of a good, thick gauge. The one illustrated in figure 1 is suitable for one tethered bird.

A weathering should be designed in such a way that it is easily cleaned out. You should be careful to protect it from digging-vermin such as foxes. It is important that it is sited so that the bird has something reasonably interesting to focus on during the day – for example the full length of the garden. A bird will quickly become bored if it faces a solid brick wall, and this could result in feather plucking.

Figure 1   A modern day weathering

Construction
The materials required for construction can normally be purchased from a large DIY warehouse. The overall construction cost should be no more than £130. You will need someone to help you, and from start to finish it should take no longer than a weekend to complete.

The materials needed to construct a weathering

- 3 6ft larch-lap standard garden fence panels
- 4 3in x 3in x 7ft garden fence posts
- 60ft 2in x 2in sawn timber
- 12ft 1in x 1in sawn timber
- 2 bitumen coated roofing boards
- 1 roll roofing felt (mineral finish)
- 1 sturdy padlock and bolt
- 8 bags of pea shingle
- 2 bags of soft sand
- 1 bag of cement
- 6sq ft 1in x 1in heavy-duty wire mesh
- Staple clips
- Selection of wide-headed clout nails
- Selection of nails
- Selection of screws
- 3 door hinges

The body of the weathering is made from the larch-lap fencing panels. Once you have marked out exactly where it will be situated, you will need to dig a hole in each of the four corners and sink the fence posts approximately 6 inches. Using a spirit level, make sure they are reasonably vertical before filling in the holes with cement. You can now screw the panels to the posts, one at the back and one on each side. Do not scrimp on the number of screws you use; the more the better. There is no need to wait until the cement has set before you do this.

To construct the front, you will need to cut and screw a length of 2in x 2in sawn timber and fix it to the inside of the front posts, at the top. This will give the construction a degree of strength. Do exactly the same to the bottom. Now fix a length of 2in x 2in sawn timber centrally between the top and bottom cross members, thus dividing the front of the weathering in half. Now make the door frame, using 2in x 2in sawn timber and making sure it fits exactly into one half of the front of the weathering. Attach the mesh to the frame and hinge the completed door into place. Cut the 1in x 1in sawn timber to size and screw it to the outer frame to make door stops. It is important that you have stops to prevent the door from swinging inwards towards the bird. Then mesh the rest of the front of the weathering.

You can now concentrate on the roof. Take approximately 6ft of the 2in x 2in sawn timber, then, using a jig saw, cut it from corner to corner, diagonally, before fixing it to the top of each side panel using screws. This will give the roof its slope. Place another length of 2in x 2in sawn timber along the back panel to even off. Again using a jig saw, cut the boards to size making sure the front section overhangs the weathering by approximately 6 inches. Screw the boards to the weathering, and finish off by felting the roof. You could either use hot bitumen to stick the felt, or clout nails, which are far easier.

Once you have checked the weathering to ensure it is watertight, you can line the bottom. Although there are many materials you could use for this, pea shingle is by far the best. Once the shingle has been laid, approximately 3 to 4 inches deep, give it a thorough hosing down to wash away the sand particles, as sand will discolour a bird's feet, tail and primary feathers.

Because larch-lap is a rather cheap material, you may find that after a while the panels begin to droop, which will allow cold draughts to circulate inside the weathering. Felting the outside will not only solve this problem, it will also give the panels more protection from the rain. Treating the panels is not an option, as you should not use creosote around a bird of prey.

It is vitally important to prevent foxes from digging their way into the weathering. Urban foxes are abundant and they will seize any opportunity to get to your bird. The easiest protection is to lay 12in x 12in paving slabs around the outside of the building.

You may like to paint the mesh; if so black is the obvious colour. It will not only look better, it will make it far easier to see the occupant inside. Any anti-rust paint will do.

A weathering of this size will accommodate most birds successfully – certainly any species that a beginner will be keeping. All birds except smaller owls should be tethered when inside, as a weathering of this size is far too small to allow a hawk free flight.

Security

Bird Theft
The theft of birds of prey is a major cause for concern. Since 1989, a national register of birds stolen from captivity has been kept. Each year the number has risen, and during 1994, following the deregistration of many species, the total stolen rose by over 20 per cent on the figures for 1993. Species that had never been stolen before, such as red-headed merlins, sooty falcons, African goshawks and tawny eagles are now being taken. The criminal element quickly realised that if ringing and registering of these birds was no longer required they could easily keep them in their back gardens knowing that government checks would no longer be made on them. The rings could be removed, since the birds were no longer subject to Schedule 4. Moreover, if the authorities did get to see them, in most cases it would be impossible to retrace their history.

The most popular bird being stolen is the Harris hawk. Over 100 have been stolen in the past three or four years. And they are no longer stealing the odd one at a time. The thieves wait until the breeding season and then steal both the parent birds and the offspring they are rearing – up to five birds at a time.

Birds are usually stolen in one of three ways. The first is a direct attack on weatherings in back gardens and falconry centres. The most common way of carrying the birds off is by stuffing them into a sack. Weatherings are, in the main, very easy to break into, and someone experienced at handling birds can be in and out in a very short time.

The second is by calling down a bird that is being flown by a falconer. This occurs mainly with falcons, which fly to great heights on thermals and wait for the falconer to bring out the lure. The bird will then come down and chase the lure as it would a real bird. A falcon will fly to anyone who is swinging the lure. There have been several occasions when a bird has been called down by a thief who is three or four fields away from the owner. The bird is allowed to catch the lure immediately, and the transmitter is removed and discarded.

The final method relates to lost birds. Many falcons and some hawks are lost whilst they are being flown. Many of them are never seen again, but many are recovered. They are found by the public and handed in at falconry centres, RSPCA hospitals, veterinary surgeries and licensed rehabilitation keepers, and are normally returned to their owners. Most bird sanctuaries or hospitals are quite honest, but experience has shown that some are not so trustworthy. There have been cases of lost hawks being taken to such places, where all identification has been removed and the hawk has been kept.

Registration Schemes

Following deregistration, a number of people started up private schemes to enable keepers to continue to register birds that had been removed from Schedule 4. Registration documents are issued, similar to those of DEFRA, and rings issued. Two such schemes are the Independent Bird Register (IBR) and Raptor Registration (RR).

Lost, Found and Stolen Birds

The Independent Bird Register also helps keepers to reclaim lost birds and try and trace owners of found birds, as does an organisation called Raptor Lifeline. Both organisations have been running since 1995 and have, to date, reunited nearly 200 birds with their owners. If you lose a bird or have one handed in it is well worth reporting it. Raptor Lifeline, run by Paul and Lyn Beecroft, can be reached by phoning or faxing 0118 9016990, and the Independent Bird Register by phoning 0870 224 7820.

PC Paul Beecroft of Thames Valley Police also collates information about birds of prey that are stolen from captivity. The register he maintains is used by all UK police forces and some EU ones. A large number of stolen birds have been recovered in the past via this register. If you have a bird stolen you should report it.

Weathering Security

Security against bird theft is always a difficult problem. Entry into a weathering is usually simplicity itself owing to the materials used in its construction. Moreover, many weatherings are situated at some distance from the house, which adds to the problem.

There are, however, a number of things that can be done. The main object of any thief is to be in and out as soon as possible, making the minimum of noise. The most obvious security feature is an alarm. There are systems to suit all requirements, including alarm bells that are situated inside the house so that they do not panic the bird. The obvious drawback is the cost; some systems can be very expensive.

Closed-circuit TV would be ideal, but it is not something everyone can afford. However, there are now dummy systems on the market costing approximately £20 which can act as a very good deterrent. Movement detector lights can also be useful. No thief wants to be in the spotlight, so to speak. But they need to be sited high enough so that the thief cannot easily knock them out.

Heavy-duty padlocks on doors are also a hindrance, especially those designed so that they cannot be bolt-cropped. Of course, the wire mesh can easily be cut, but this will take far longer. Another good idea is gravel paths. The noise of someone walking on gravel, especially at night, is quite loud and most dogs will hear it even if you do not.

One simple alarm system that can be very cheaply installed but is extremely effective consists only of a fishing line and a bell. The line is strategically placed across the front of the weathering about one foot from the ground and led into the house, where a bell is attached.

There is one other thing that falconers can do to improve security, and that is to avoid 'loose talk'. I have often overheard conversations between falconers, in which they talk about their birds, what they are, how good the breeding season was etc. About the only thing they have not revealed is their ring numbers. You must be cautious about what you say and in whose presence. Birds of prey are more often than not stolen by other keepers or agents working for them. The only people that are interested in these birds are other keepers themselves, and in virtually all cases of theft, the victim has either known the culprit or has had a friend who has known him.

Microchips

A microchip or microtag is an injectable passive transponder which provides an electronic means of identification. The miniature transponder is approximately the size of a grain of rice. It is protected by special glass which, when it is inserted into an animal or bird, becomes virtually impossible to remove except by means of an operation. The transponder does not require a battery. It is activated by a reader and it transmits its own unique code number, which is in turn displayed on the reader.

There are two types of reader, the static and the portable or mobile. Static readers are generally found at veterinary surgeries, RSPCA hospitals etc. They are widely used by vets and you should not have too much difficulty obtaining access to one. Portable readers are also normally held by vets, and also by RSPCA inspectors, RSPB investigation officers, DEFRA officials and some police officers.

There are three microchip companies operating in Great Britain, and their full addresses can be found in the Appendix. RS Biotech who use the Trovan system, Pettrac the Avid system and Animalcare the Identichip system. The Trovan system has not been widely used in birds of prey. It also has the disadvantage that the Trovan reader will not read the other companies' chips and vice versa. Avid and Identichip have both been used in large numbers in birds of prey, and each company's reader will read the chips of the other.

CHAPTER THREE

Equipment

Before buying your first bird of prey or owl, you must acquire a vast array of suitable equipment. Few of the items can be made at home, particularly by a novice, who is unlikely to have the right product knowledge. However, most good falconry courses will show you how to make items such as anklets, jesses and bewitts, although they will not go into other items such as hoods, gloves, bags, swivels, bells and perches etc.

There are distinct advantages in purchasing the highest calibre of equipment. As with most products, cheapness is often associated with poor quality. Second-rate equipment may seem attractive, but it is false economy, as it will not last.

This section concentrates on the equipment a falconer needs to train and maintain a bird of prey. All prices are approximate and do not take into account postage and packaging.

Equipment check

- 1 glove or gauntlet
- 1 bag
- 1 perch
- 1 hood, if applicable
- 2 swivels
- 1 pair of bells
- 1 creance
- 1 lure
- 2 leashes
- 1 hawk bath
- 1 set of field jesses
- 1 set of mews jesses
- 1 set of anklets
- 1 pair of bewitts
- 1 set of quality scales
- telemetry system
- sundries: grease, whistle, feather straightener, set of closing tools, leather punch, set of needle files

Size
Suppliers' catalogues will generally have a guide to size. This is vitally important as it will help you determine the correct size of equipment

for your bird. A supplier will also ask you to indicate the species of bird, its gender and if possible a flying weight with your order. This is to double check that the equipment intended is compatible and suited to your bird.

The guide to size will not itemise every known species of bird of prey or owl, but only those that are most common among today's practising falconers. If your particular bird is not displayed, telephone the supplier for further information. Below is the guide we use at the Eagle-Owl School of Falconry.

M = Male. F = Female.

Small: Sparrowhawk, Merlin, Kestrel, Little Owl, etc.

Medium: Barn Owl, Tawny Owl, M. Falcons, M. Goshawk, M. Buzzard, M. Harris Hawk, etc.

Large: F. Falcons, F. Goshawk, F. Harris Hawk, M. Red-tail, M. Ferruginous, etc.

Extra large: F. Ferruginous, F. Red-tail, Snowy Owl, European Eagle-owl, etc.

I suggest that you visit a supplier if possible rather than order over the telephone or via post, as you will be entering into an area of falconry which is fraught with potential dangers. For instance, bells may seem reasonably priced and be referred to as having a very good tone. If you order by post, you are not in a position to judge for yourself. If they fall below your expectations you will then have the annoying inconvenience of sending them back and waiting for either an alternative variety or your money back. Being able to see and hear what you are buying, and compare quality is invaluable, and I would strongly recommend a beginner to buy in person at least until he is familiar with certain makes of equipment and suppliers.

The best way for a beginner to purchase equipment is to visit the falconry fair. This is held annually and is advertised in the *Falconer's Magazine* and *Cage and Aviary Birds*. Held over two days, it is a must for all falconers with many suppliers available to advise and assess your needs. You can then compare quality, design and price. Attending the fair and buying a full range of equipment from one supplier may even make you eligible for a discount. There are also excellent flying displays throughout the day, with many experienced falconers at hand to answer your questions. It is unique in Great Britain and well worth a visit.

But however you acquire your equipment, make sure you do not rush into your decision. Take time and care before parting with any money.

Falconry Gloves/Gauntlets

Falconry gloves or gauntlets are designed to serve two purposes. First, they give the falconer protection from a bird's sharp, powerful talons, which could cause serious wounds if they were to embed themselves in the skin, and secondly they act as a cushion for the bird's feet whilst it is being carried for long periods of time. You may occasionally see falconers picking their hawks up without any protection. This is foolish, but it is something we all do from time to time, probably without thinking. However, even the smallest birds can inflict nasty wounds which are totally avoidable.

A falconry glove must be a perfect fit. It should be tough but with enough suppleness for ease of finger movement. It must feel comfortable, give the correct degree of protection and be finished to a high standard. Although the design is not particularly important, you should take pride in the appearance of your equipment just as you should in your bird. You will therefore need a glove that is reasonably attractive. All gloves should have either a hanging tassel or brass D-ring, so you have something safe to attach the leash to. Most gloves however come with both.

Falconry gloves are available in various lengths and thicknesses to accommodate the many different sizes of bird; the normal sizes are wrist-length, mid-length and full-length. They will have either a single or a double layer of leather to provide protection against gripping talons. Some may have three layers, but this will obviously reduce their flexibility. A wrist-length, single-thickness gauntlet would be suitable for small birds such as kestrels or merlins, but would not give you the protection you need with birds such as hawks, medium to large owls and falcons, where you would require either a mid-length or full-length, double-thickness gauntlet. They are made from a variety of leathers, including elk and deer hide. Most suppliers will ask you to supply a hand drawing on ordering to ensure as close a fit as possible.

Gloves vary tremendously in price. A wrist-length, single-thickness one will cost approximately £25, a mid-length, double-thickness one approximately £35, and a full-length, double-thickness one approximately £45. Gloves below these prices are cheap and probably low-quality, while any which cost more are becoming rather expensive; unless they are made from a top-quality leather such as deer skin, I would suggest you look elsewhere. You may find that certain suppliers make a surcharge on gloves that are very small or very large. If you need such gloves, you should add approximately 15–20 per cent to the above prices.

A falconry gauntlet will need to be adequately maintained to achieve maximum usage. Never wash your glove with soap and water as it will cause the pores to deteriorate and harden the leather. Dirty gloves should be cleaned in a rapid motion using a medium-course brush. You should wax your glove as soon as it is purchased, and continue treating the leather at regular intervals. If it should get wet, hang it up to dry, but never around artificial heat.

Some gauntlets are available with the interior lined with sheepskin. This can be an asset when the weather is at its coldest. The gloved hand tends not to move too much and will therefore always feel colder. An additional glove of this design is well worth having amongst your equipment.

Falconry Bags and Waistcoats

Falconry bags are rarely cleaned or maintained. They are dragged and forced through brambles, bushes etc. and spend much of the time damp, and are generally not treated with any degree of respect, so they need to be robust. They are designed to take items of equipment, captured quarry and pieces of meat for recalling a bird back to the fist.

The way in which some bags are finished often falls below the standard required. Over the years I have scratched my knuckles countless times when digging around inside the pockets because the canvas has not been adequately folded and stitched, and it therefore has sharp edges. On a cold winter's day this can be most annoying and quite uncomfortable.

There are certain design features you should bear in mind when buying a bag. A good bag will be strong, fairly flexible, and finished to a high standard. The stitching should be neat and smooth, as it is this which is normally the first casualty on a cheaper bag. When the stitching deteriorates, the bag gradually falls apart.

Most falconry bags have handy little pockets. These are ideal for spare swivels and whistles, and most importantly a small first-aid kit. Very few falconers carry first-aid kits, which surprises me. If your bird is bitten by a squirrel, for instance, it will need immediate attention, rather than waiting until you get back to the car. (For more on first-aid kits, see pages 129-131.)

The main pocket, often called the game pocket, must be of a size to accommodate at least a couple of rabbits, and have no internal pockets. The second major pocket is used to carry lures, the creance and a spare leash or two. This pocket should contain a detachable meat pouch. It is important that the pouch is detachable as it will need to be thoroughly cleaned and sterilised after use. It is also a good idea to check that the pouch is large enough to accommodate your hand. They are often long and very narrow, which can make it hard work trying to dig around inside for small pieces of meat.

Most bags will have either two or four brass eyelets embedded in one of the pocket flaps or alternatively in pieces of leather which are

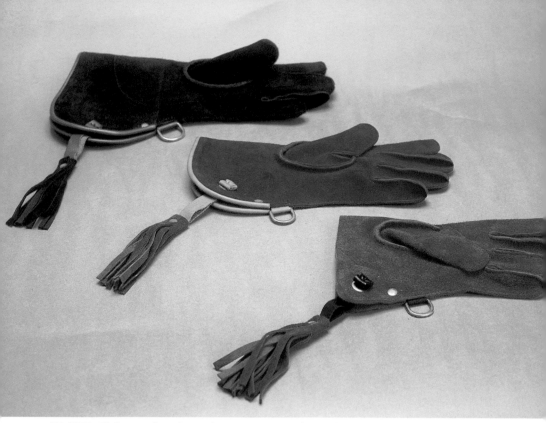

ABOVE: *Falconry gloves/gauntlets.* BELOW: *Falconry bags*

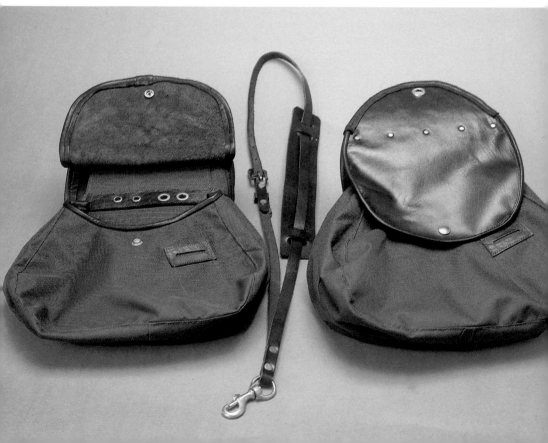

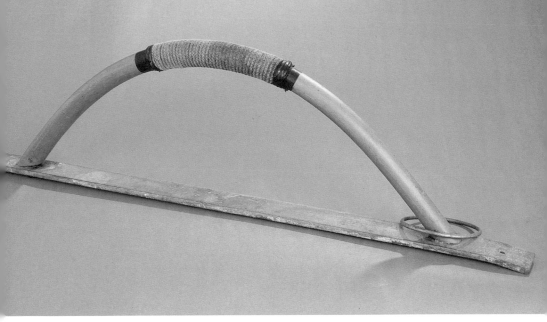

ABOVE: *A bow perch*
BELOW: *A block perch*

BELOW: *A creance*

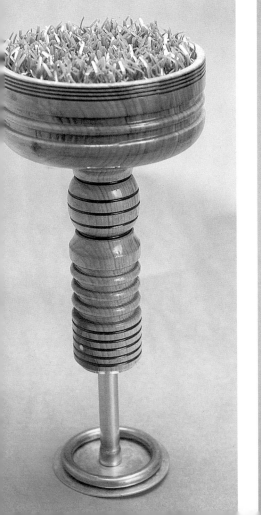

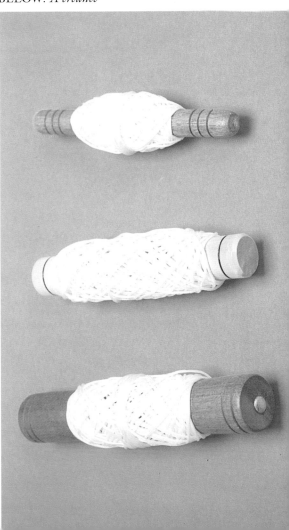

then stitched onto the bag. These are for spare jesses.

When ordering a falconry bag from a supplier, you must also order either a strap or a belt, as these are classed as separate items. Some suppliers only stock straps. The swivel mechanism which allows you to spin freely from game to storage pocket is normally found on the strap or belt, very rarely on the bag.

Some suppliers stock leather bags, which are mainly used for those conducting flying displays. They are very elegant, but can be twice the price of the average canvas bag, so they are not the kind of thing to be mistreated in the field. Many suppliers will give you the choice of a small or a large bag. Choose the larger as it will have a bigger game pocket, although the smaller ones are fine when you are manning and training your bird.

A well-made, practical falconry bag will cost approximately £40, and a strap or belt £10–15.

Many falconers today have ceased to use bags, however, and now have flying waistcoats. A good waistcoat will have the same number of pockets and attachments as a bag, and should be just as hardy and versatile. A number of my friends made the change to waistcoats and persevered for many months before reverting back to the bag. Personally I have found them restricting and rather uncomfortable to wear, but they may suit you, so keep your options open and try both.

Very few suppliers stock waistcoats, so you may find they are a little difficult to obtain. The falconry fair is the best place to find one, and you can expect to pay the same price as you would for a good, large hawking bag.

Bow Perches

Bow perches are available in small, medium and large sizes. They are normally manufactured in one of three ways: mild steel, which is then painted or sprayed using an anti-rusting agent; mild steel that is insulated in pipe tubing; and stainless steel.

Outdoor bows have spikes that have to be pushed into the ground to keep the frame sturdy. They will be finished off in either leather or cord binding, to provide the perching and gripping surface for the hawk. Most suppliers only stock bows with one kind of perching surface. Some falconers prefer their birds to stand on Astroturf, as it has been proved to help prevent bumblefoot (see pages 126-7). You will find that very few suppliers finish their bows in this surface, so you may have to ask for it to be done, or else attempt it yourself.

Bow perches are designed to accommodate hawks, buzzards and large owls. The curve is intended to simulate the branch of a tree; in the wild, these species would spend a great deal of time perched in trees. Beginners frequently attempt to make their own bows, rarely with any great success, and often these versions are positively dangerous.

When looking at bow perches, be prepared for many weird and wonderful designs, but be sure that you do not choose looks above quality. A bow must also be the correct size for your bird. It would be silly to put a female red-tail on a bow designed for a sparrowhawk, as her tail feathers would trail the ground and the padded gripping section would not be thick enough for her massive feet. The tethering ring must be large enough to slip back and forth easily over the padded perching surface so that it does not tangle. The general appearance of the perch must be tidy and the welding, which is what holds the structure together, finished to a high standard.

Stainless steel bows are by far the best. Although they are expensive, they are strong, will not rust, will give years of use and will be practically maintenance-free. Mild steel bows with an anti-rusting agent will also have a long life, but the metal will need to be repainted regularly as the movement of the ring will cause the paint to peel. They tend to look old and tatty after only a short period. Mild steel bows finished in pipe tubing are cheaper than stainless steel ones, and are also virtually maintenance-free and will look attractive for many a season.

Whatever type you purchase, make absolutely sure that the tethering ring is made from stainless steel or brass. Do not settle for anything else. Because of the strength of stainless steel, the Tig weld which is a cleaner method of fusing two metals together, will be extremely unlikely to snap. Brass is acceptable, but you must bear in mind that it will wear far more quickly than stainless steel. Tethering rings made from mild steel must always be avoided.

Indoor bows have no spikes. Instead they have heavy-duty solid plates or tubes welded onto each end. This design is ideal when the ground is very hard or you have a base where spikes would prove impracticable. The indoor bow is also much more versatile than the outdoor one, as it is a perch for all occasions. Although it is a little dearer, it may be a better proposition when you are starting out.

I believe that all falconers should have a suitable indoor perch. They enable you to bring a bird that is unwell inside overnight, which could save her life.

A small mild-steel, outdoor bow will cost approximately £25, a medium one £30 and a large one £40. Expect to pay a little more for one finished in plastic tubing. For stainless steel perches you should add approximately 60 per cent to these prices. Indoor bows cost about 15 per cent more than outdoor ones.

Block Perches
The construction of a block perch gives me endless pleasure. One experiences a therapeutic feeling from watching a piece of timber spinning at great speeds on a lathe as it is transformed into something

of real beauty.

Block perches are designed to accommodate small to medium-sized owls and falcons. They have a flat perching surface which is intended to simulate the natural surface which these species would be familiar with in the wild. Like bows, they are available in small, medium and large sizes. The perching surface will consist of either Astroturf or cork. Few suppliers finish their blocks in leather.

A variety of hardwoods are used in the manufacturing of blocks, including mahogany, elm, walnut, oak, sycamore and cherry. All are distinctive, and each has its own beauty. Personally, I have found Brazilian mahogany to be an excellent wood and we now use nothing else for our perches. There is a consistency in its raw state which leads to less wastage. We have found that it turns very well on the lathe, as it maintains a tight, consistent grain. Although it is a natural dark wood with limited grain, its beauty is evident after three coats of clear protective lacquer. But most importantly, once treated, it weathers extremely well. However, all these woods have their own distinctive grain patterns and characteristics, and are all adequate for block construction.

I have come across blocks that have been turned from softwood, stained to resemble mahogany or walnut and finished to a standard where a layman would not know the difference. But blocks made in this way will not withstand the effects of harsh winters and will consequently be a waste of money. They are not common, but you should be aware that they exist.

It is vital that a block perch should be strong and well made with the wooden body and round top thoroughly sanded and smooth to prevent your bird from receiving splinters. Beginners should not attempt their own, as there are too many important design and safety elements to be taken into account. The internal construction must be strong, as this is where 50 per cent of the problems arise.

There are two internal designs I recommend. The first has a small hole recessed a third of the way into the under part of the wooden stem (see figure 2). This is to accommodate a length of

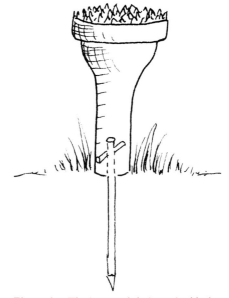

Figure 2   The internal design of a block perch, with the rod hole recessed

stainless steel rod. The tip of the rod will also have a small hole drilled through it, approximately one inch from the end, the same size as the hole in the stem of the block. The rod is glued and pushed into the block, making sure that its hole is lined up with the hole in the stem. A thick brass or stainless steel pin is then inserted into the block, through the stainless steel rod and out on the other side. Once the glue has hardened off, the pin is filed flush with the side of the stem. You now have a perch that is extremely strong, and the rod will not fall out when it is removed from hard ground.

The second design is slightly different (see figure 3). A small hole has again been drilled vertically into the under part of the wooden stem, but this time it runs through the whole length of the block and through the round perching top. The tip of the stainless steel rod has approximately one inch of thread applied to the end, which allows it to be fixed with a sturdy nut. This is another totally safe design.

Both styles are known as Arabic-style blocks. I like this design. It is almost impossible for the bird to foul the stem of the perch since it is well protected, being much slimmer than the larger top. Block perches that are manufactured in either of these ways are also the most secure on

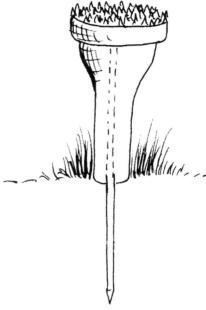

Figure 3   The internal design of a block perch, with the rod hole drilled right through the stem and top

the market. The keys to a good block perch are good-quality wood, stainless steel metalwork, and an anti-tangle system, which prevents the leash from getting snagged up around the block's metalwork.

The designs for indoor blocks are almost identical, the only difference being the weighted bottom, which will be a solid round plate. Like indoor bows, indoor blocks are perches for all occasions.

Prices are similar to those of outdoor and indoor bows whether constructed from mild or stainless steel.

Creance
The word 'creance' is French and means 'a piece of string'. This 'piece of string', however, is the most vital item of equipment in your bird's training.

A creance is a hardwood stick around which is wound a suitable line. It is customary to wind the line with one hand, in figure-of-eight rotations. This technique should be practised continually until you get it right. It will eliminate the possibility of knots and tangles occurring, which can quite easily happen when you have up to 50 yards of fine line. It also allows you to hold a bird safely whilst you are doing it.

The creance is a safety aid whilst you are teaching a bird to fly to a garnished fist. The stick or handle is shaped on a lathe in a variety of designs which enable you to gather the line in neatly, efficiently and quickly.

They are available in three sizes – small, medium and large – which determine the overall weight of the finished item. Most suppliers will give you the choice of either 25 or 50 yards of braided nylon or Terylene line.

Before each training session, you should be certain that no part of the line has started to fray. This could lead to it eventually snapping and allowing the untrained bird to fly free and possibly become snagged in a tree by her swivel and trailing line.

Once a bird is jumping the full length of the leash, you must immediately exchange it for a creance. To do this, detach the leash and tie the line to the lower eye of the swivel, using a falconer's knot (see page 64). During each training session you will be asking your bird to fly a little further to accept her reward. There is no rush and you must never ask a bird to do too much too quickly, or you run the risk of her flying straight over your head, as her nervousness outweighs the desire for food. A bird should not overshoot the fist; if she does she will have to be pulled down as smoothly as possible using the creance. Although this is the only method of bringing a bird safely under control, it risks injuring her legs. You should therefore let her progress at a sensible pace and make sure there are no tempting trees immediately behind you. Once a bird has come to the end of the line, the creance is then discarded, as the next step is for her to be set loose.

Although one should never rush a hawk whilst it is on the creance, beginners often hold their first hawk back too long. Some birds spend most of the season restricted to a training line as their owners are afraid of letting them fly free. Some birds, especially falcons, learn very quickly, and this is where the ability to assess your bird's progression comes into play. A hawk maintained on a creance for too long will soon become bored with the same monotonous routine and you may affect her potential when you do finally gain the confidence to allow her to fly free. Most falconers hate the restriction of the creance and will work extra hard with their bird in an attempt to discard it as quickly as possible; the sooner the bird is flying free, the sooner one can work on her fitness.

A small creance will cost approximately £7.50, a medium one £9.50 and a large one £12.

Swivels

Many beginners fail to appreciate how important a good swivel is. Even if you have to settle for a cheaper glove or falconry bag, I cannot stress too strongly how vital it is not to settle for second best when purchasing a swivel.

This is the item that secures the jesses and the leash. It has to withstand immense pulling pressure both top and bottom. If a bird bates from her perch, the jesses pull the upper section whilst the heat-sealed button at the top of the leash pulls the lower. Although it is rare, it has been known for inadequate swivels to snap under this kind of pressure. If this happens, you will possibly have lost your bird.

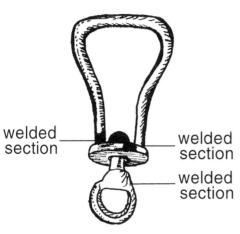

Figure 4 The welded sections of swivels

welded section

welded section

welded section

Swivels are available in a variety of designs. As with all items of equipment, provided they are safe and made to an adequate standard, choose the one you find attractive. After all, nice-looking and well-maintained equipment will enhance your bird's general appearance. Although a picture in a catalogue cannot show you the quality, you will get a very good idea of the design. If you like what you see, contact the supplier to clarify any queries you may have about the construction. If you are not completely satisfied when you receive them, you will find that most suppliers have a policy of either replacing items or accepting goods back for a full refund.

Although swivels may appear rather expensive, a lot of work is involved in their manufacturing. Stainless steel swivels can only be made by people with the ability to work with this tricky metal. Whilst it is being shaped, it is very easy for it to snap. The price of stainless steel being what it is, this is something one cannot afford to allow to happen too often. The construction entails the shaping, grinding and welding of many small pieces. This is very time-consuming and a skill that must not be rushed. And once the swivel is complete, it is polished to enhance its appearance. Very few people have the ability to work in stainless steel to this kind of standard, and those who can are highly skilled tradesmen, hence the price.

Stainless steel swivels are not made in one continuous strip of metal. They consist of pieces which are shaped, and welded together (see figure 4). Although any form of welding should be stronger than the metal itself, there are weak points that may snap if they are not welded properly.

Stainless steel swivels are the most popular, and probably the best available. As I have said, stainless steel is immensely tough and if it is Tig-welded to a professional standard, there is virtually no danger of it snapping. You can also buy brass swivels, but although they are considerably cheaper than stainless steel, brass is a much softer metal, and will wear in time. Brass swivels should be kept spotlessly clean or they will turn green, and this will result in the metal wearing far sooner. Some swivels are chrome plated; again they will be cheaper than stainless steel, but they are not as good. You run the risk of rusting occurring if they are not plated correctly.

A good swivel will be designed in such a way as to prevent the jesses and leash from becoming tangled. The lower ring should spin smoothly and without interference. Although no swivel can be guaranteed not to allow a bird to become tangled, a well-designed one will certainly reduce the chances. It is important that you get the right-sized swivel for your bird. If it is too small it may not have the strength to withstand the pressure that will be exerted on it and it will also not accommodate the jesses, as they will be far too bulky. If it is too large, the bird will be uncomfortable and look unbalanced, and it will add unnecessary weight to her legs whilst she is tethered to the perch.

Stainless steel swivels are available in small, medium, large and extra large sizes, and cost approximately £5, £7.50, £10 and £12 respectively. Brass and chrome-plated swivels cost approximately 30 per cent less.

Swivels

Swing lures

Swing Lures

The lure pad, or swing lure as it is often called, is an item of training equipment. It is designed for longwings, shortwings and broadwings. As the falconer swings the lure in a backward rotation, the bird is encouraged to chase and finally catch it in mid-air to receive a reward in the form of a portion of meat securely attached to the pad by a length of string. The lure is also an effective way of encouraging a stubborn bird to leave a cosy tree and return to the ground, and can be invaluable if you lose your bird. You can scout a wide area of land swinging the lure and blowing your whistle. Many lost birds are recovered in this way.

Before you begin swinging the lure towards a bird, however, you must first allow yourself a good week or two of intense practice. The swing lure is a means of developing a bird of prey's natural ability to chase and kill. If it is swung incorrectly you can easily injure the bird and make her lure-shy.

A good lure swinger will give the bird every opportunity of catching. The pad is rotated slowly and the bird turns in to make a grab, believing it is live quarry. Then, just as the talons protrude, the pad is pulled through and away from the bird. This is known as passing; there are a number of ways in which to pass a hawk, but what is called the side pass is by far the easiest to master when beginning. You must swing the lure at a sensible pace to encourage your bird to chase. If you rotate it too quickly and aggressively, you will give your hawk no chance, and she may 'blank' the lure altogether, believing it is not within her ability to catch.

Lure pads are available in three sizes – small, medium and large – and it is imperative that you order the correct size for your bird. It should be as light and as soft as possible; if it is too heavy, like those that are packed with sand, it may hurt or bruise her feet when she catches it in mid-air.

The bodies of most lures are of a standard design, and are made from soft leather skins and packed, usually with toy filling. They have a small swivel mechanism which prevents them from tangling with the line whilst they are being rotated. You will also need a lure stick, which will normally come complete with around 10 feet of thickish line. The weight and size of the lure stick should be right for the pad and the species of bird it is intended for. You must also be sure that the line is thick enough not to cut into your hand whilst it is being swung, but more importantly, not to cut into the bird if it makes any contact with her.

Wings that have been professionally cured are placed on the pad. You can choose which you want from a wide variety, from sparrow to pheasant, to familiarise your hawk with the coloration of any particular quarry. One important thing to look for when purchasing a swing lure is the way the wings are to be attached. You will probably find that to one side of the pad there are two small cable ties, which are intended to hold the wings firmly in place. Once the wings are placed in position, you trim the ties to reduce their length. The problem with this method is there are always sharp edges, which could cause terrible abrasions to a bird's feet. If the pad you order has cable ties – and most do – remove them immediately and replace them with string. This will be much safer.

Some falconers do not use lure pads at all if they are flying a small bird such as a kestrel, as the risk of damage to the feet on impact is too great. If you are worried about this, you could tie a pair of wings back to back, using the meat not only as the reward but also to give the pad suitable weight.

The complete swing lure kit, comprising a pad, wings and a lure stick with line, will cost approximately £10 for the small size, £12 for the medium and £15 for the large.

Rabbit Lures

Rabbit lures are designed for shortwings and broadwings. It is customary not to show them to longwings, as they are generally trained to seize flying, feathered game. In Great Britain, it is illegal to use live quarry for the purpose of training birds of prey so a dummy is used. Although some people see this as a great disadvantage, your bird will soon come to realise what the lure is intended to simulate and will eventually be eager to kill.

When you feel the time is right, and your bird is ready, introduce her to the rabbit lure. The way in which you do this and the timing, are vitally important to the continuation of progress. Some people stand within two or three feet of their bird and rotate the lure in the same way as they would a swing lure. This is asking for trouble, as it will only frighten the bird and make your job much harder. It is far better to fix the rabbit lure firmly in the weathering before tethering your bird inside for the night. Make sure it is adequately garnished and well within striking distance of the bird. By morning, the food will be gone and your bird will have been introduced to this daunting item of equipment. After a few nights, you will be in a position to start the lure training properly.

The bird may jump from her perch and land to one side of the lure before gingerly skipping over to within pecking distance. It is important not to allow her to steal a piece in this way. Instead, pull the lure slowly towards you. Hopefully she will thrust out a foot to hold it steady. If she does, continue to pull it until she puts both feet completely on it, then stop pulling and let her receive the reward. Always garnish the lure well in the early stages to encourage her. Given time, she will develop the confidence to leave her perch and fly directly onto the lure.

When she flies and binds onto her first live rabbit, however, it will not sit motionless; it will put up a struggle. Once she is confident, therefore, gradually try to simulate this activity whilst she is on the lure.

There is no doubt that an enormous amount of skill is involved in using both swing and rabbit lures, just as there is when encouraging a young bird to eat off the fist for the first time. But even the most stubborn of young hawks can be encouraged to fly the lure, and often it is just a case of knowing when and when not to twitch the line. Like many aspects of falconry, this cannot easily be taught. Until you have served a long apprenticeship you will develop these skills by trial and error.

The rabbit lure should be of a good size – about that of a small rabbit. The body must be thick and contain soft padding, which will give maximum protection to the bird's feet. It should resemble a rabbit, although some do not. It should have a light-coloured tail, preferably white, and the head end should be a flat piece of robust leather. Short lengths of string on either side of the head section will allow you to tie meat securely onto it.

You should never use cable ties to attach the bird's reward, as they

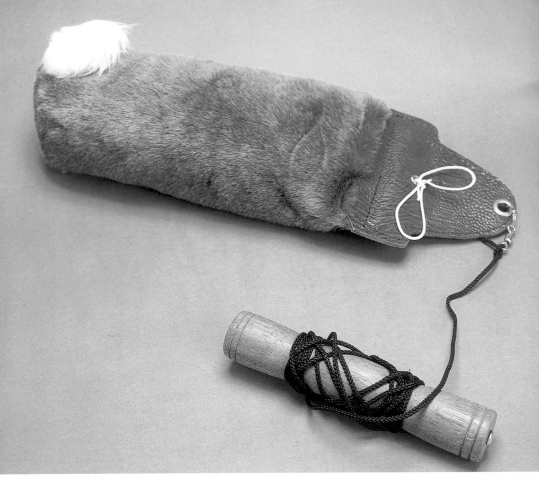

A rabbit lure

could cause the same problems as in swing lures. Check the leather sections regularly for sharp points, as they could injure your bird's feet. You must always tie the bird's reward towards the head end of the lure as eventually, when she is hunting, you will want her to attack the head of the quarry rather than tentatively hitting the hind quarters.

I like to introduce a hawk to the rabbit lure as soon as possible. However, make sure you do not frighten her by being over-enthusiastic. If you attend a good falconry course, you will be given all the relevant information on how and when to introduce the rabbit lure.

Some falconers prefer to use dummy pads which are designed for training hunt, point and retrieve dogs. These are canvas pads which are covered in a cured rabbit skin or artificial fur. Whatever design you choose, make sure the hawk can differentiate between head and tail.

The rabbit lure kit consists of a rabbit lure pad, a lure stick and line. You will find there is only one size offered by suppliers, and it will cost approximately £16.

Hoods

The hooding of a raptor is a very important part of the training process, and it must be done with a high degree of dexterity.

I am often asked at shows whether hooding a bird is cruel. I only hood falcons at shows, and my answer is that they are the thoroughbred of raptors. Like racehorses they are highly strung and can react strongly to minor disturbances. The hood calms the bird down and puts her at ease, so it is not cruel, nor should it be unpleasant for the bird if it is done correctly.

Hoods can be used on all birds except owls, which have eyes situated on the sides of their head, and I like to familiarise all my birds to the hood. But it is important that you start hood training at the correct time. Your bird should be at the stage of perching steadily and accepting food via the fist. Initially, no raptor will sit still and allow you to place the hood casually over her head. She will bate, puff her feathers, hiss, foot and even bite to keep it at bay. But she must not get the better of you, and once you have started you must do everything in your power to accomplish the task. Having said that, never overstress a bird as this could have devastating effects.

A plain Anglo-Indian hood

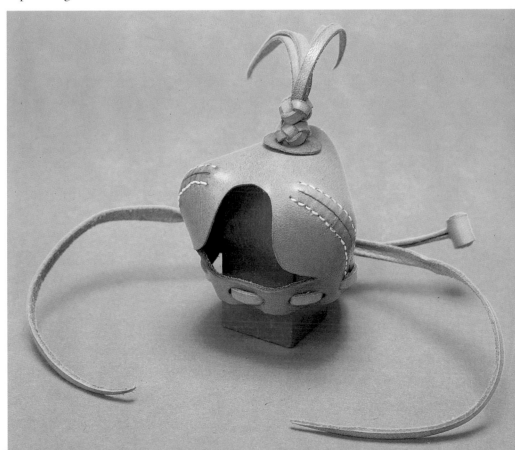

I like to leave the hood inside the weathering for two or three nights. This often makes the job of hooding much easier when the time comes. If I still have trouble, I place small pieces of food inside the hood and tempt the bird to accept the offerings. But never push the hood suddenly over her head whilst doing this as it could again have disastrous effects. Once you have built up your bird's confidence in this way, she will soon accept the hood, and regular sessions will become a pleasure.

If you intend to join broadwing and shortwing field meets, where there are other birds, you may find it necessary to hood your bird. Apart from Harris hawks, only one hawk can be slipped at any one time. If your bird has visual contact of bolting quarry, it will naturally want to take to the wing, and if it is not your slip you will have to hold her back. This will probably send her into a frenzy of bating attacks. On a large field meet, there may be up to a dozen falconers. This means your bird might have to wait a long time, and will become frustrated if she is constantly held back. She may even become unwilling to fly quarry at all. If she is hooded, however, she will not see the other flights and therefore will be none the wiser.

Moreover, a bird that has never been made to accept the hood will have to be transported in a wooden travelling box, where she could break feathers. You can put a tail sheaf onto the tail feathers to reduce the risk of damage, but I would find this a bit of a burden every time I went out hawking. It is therefore a tremendous advantage if your bird hoods. You can sit her on a travelling cadge, which greatly reduces or eliminates feather damage.

There are many hoods on the market that are quite unsuitable for putting over a bird's fragile head. A hood must be a perfect fit. If it is too large, she will see daylight, which is no good, and if it is too small, you will hurt the bird when the braces are drawn, which could make her *hood-shy*. Good hoods are expertly crafted by skilled tradesmen using top-quality leather, and are finished to an exceptionally high standard. They must be well balanced, with support in the right places, namely the girth (the piece of leather that runs below the bird's lower mandible) and around the eye sections. The stitching should be neat and smoothly tailored. I have one hood which has a protruding seam on the inside, exactly where the bird's eyes would be. This could cause unnecessary discomfort and even inflict nasty wounds to and around the eyes. Hoods designed in this way must never be used.

The hood is slipped over the bird's head using the top knot and the tips of the fingers. If it does not fall immediately into place, you can align it by gently tapping the top knot. When it is in position, the braces – the thin leather straps that open and close the back of the hood – are drawn closed. Use the tips of the fingers of your right hand (assuming the bird is carried on your left hand) and with your teeth, draw the braces together quickly and evenly. To open or strike the braces, just reverse the process. Never be heavy-handed. Remember there is a vulnerable head inside, so handle it with care at all times. Whether fully accustomed to the hood or not, a bird must never be left unattended for any period of time. She could fall from her perch and become hopelessly tangled, which could result in her death.

Some beginners try to make a hood following a pattern. Personally, I do not think it is a good idea. You will put in many hours of tedious work and probably finish up with something totally inadequate. I have tried for years, and to this day I do not have one to show off. I have failed miserably to master the fine techniques needed to produce something of a suitable standard.

There are various kinds of hood available. The cheapest is the Anglo-Indian hood, which is made from one piece of leather. That is not to say it is inadequate in any way; it is simply the easiest hood to make. It is ideal for the novice as it slips easily over the bird's head. Anglo-Indian hoods do tend to lose their shape, however, so you should keep them well padded with kitchen roll when they are not in use. Although they are also available as blocked hoods, I do not recommend a novice to use any blocked hood with a young bird.

I still use Anglo-Indian hoods for broadwings, even when the bird has come to accept the hood readily, as I find this design perfect for their heads.

Probably my favourite hood, however, is the Bahreini. It is attractive, looks comfortable and fits incredibly well. Once a longwing or shortwing accepts the hood, I move them straight onto it. It is traditionally made from one piece of leather, and the braces are threaded through a series of prepared slits at the back, which compress into neat folds when drawn. It is also available in a blocked version, and many have coloured side panels which greatly enhance the overall appearance.

The Dutch hood is made from three pieces of leather, and some are finished with a fancy feathered plume. At first glance it may appear to be rather bulky and as a consequence quite heavy but I can assure you it is not. Blocked hoods are mainly reserved for longwings. The side panels are of a different colour from the main body, and the feathered plume enhances the overall appearance. I like to use the Dutch hood at shows, as it gives my falcons added beauty.

Over the years, hoods have become incredibly fancy, and many would not look out of place in a display cabinet. These ornate designs also cost a lot of money, however, and I do not think I would use a hood that has cost well over £100. There are Dutch hoods available with hand paintings of raptors and falconry themes emblazoned onto both side panels. Although they are quite stunning and would look superb placed over a longwing's head, even *they* must still be thoroughly examined to ensure that they are suitably made.

Anglo-Indian hoods cost £15 and Bahreini ones £25 (£5 more for the blocked versions), while Dutch hoods start at £50.

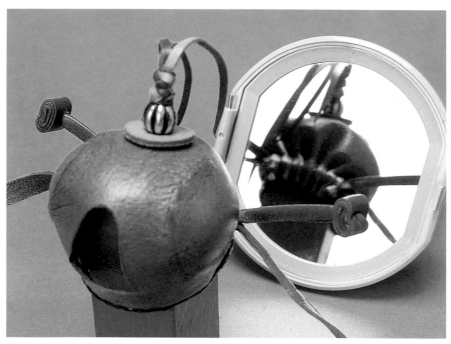

ABOVE: *A Bahreini hood*   BELOW: *A Dutch hood*

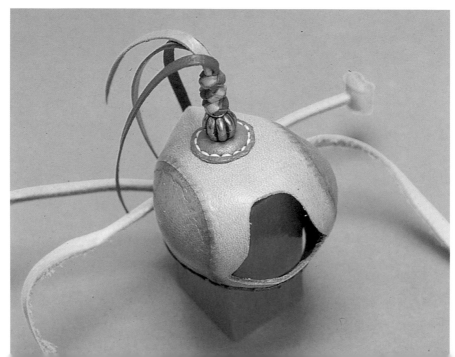

Falconry Bells

Falconry bells are essential for longwings, shortwings and broadwings, but are not necessary for owls. Indeed, many falconers believe that by attaching bells to owls you are minimising their ability to hunt, as they rely on their acute hearing and unique ability to fly practically silently whilst hunting for food. The sound of ringing bells would therefore be a hindrance, and you should think seriously before you use them on these birds.

Bells are fixed to raptors for many reasons. If a bird is temporarily lost, perhaps because she has killed out of sight, you can often locate her by their distinctive ring. Moreover, if she is sitting in a tree whilst you beat bushes to flush quarry, you can hear her every movement, which is useful if she sees a rabbit somewhere else; the bells will tell you immediately when she flies. Providing the bells are of a suitable standard, the slightest movement from the bird will send the tone travelling a very long way, especially downwind.

Bells are fixed either onto the bird's legs by means of leather bewits (see page 79) or onto the centre deck feathers. I believe the latter is the best. More and more falconers are using electric cable ties to fix them onto the legs, but I do not think this is a good idea, as the scales can easily be damaged. The attraction of the tail bell for me is tidiness – I like a bird's legs to be as free as possible. She will already have leather anklets and a registration ring to contend with; adding bells just makes the legs look more messy. The tail bell is out of the way and less likely to become tangled when the hawk is sitting

Falconry bells

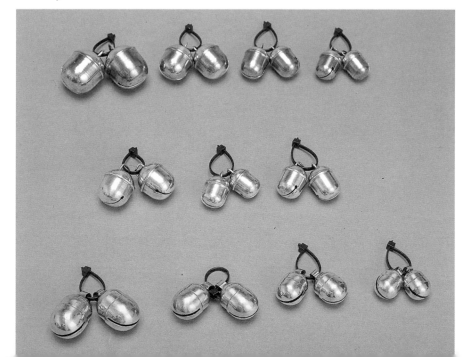

in a tree. There are various ways to attach both leg and tail bells, and you should familiarise yourself with the different methods.

Falconry bells are manufactured from a variety of materials. Brass is widely used, and is preferred by many falconers, while nickel silver is also very popular. No matter what the material is, or the appearance of the bell, the most important thing is the tone. Brass bells that are highly polished may look attractive, but they will not be very useful if the tone is not clear. There are many different makes and designs on the market. At the top end of the scale are bells from America that all seem to ring with distinctive clarity, whilst at the lower end are bells suitable only for domestic cats. The best British bell is the Titan, which is available either in brass or phosphor bronze and nickel silver. Phosphor bronze is used because of its superior toughness and wear resistance compared with brass. It also has a better resonance and a sweeter tone.

Some of the cheaper bells from Pakistan have excellent tones, but the material used will probably be thin and weak, and they are unlikely to last into the second season. However, they are ideal for a young bird that will inevitably pick and pull at her bells. They have two benefits: because they are cheaper, they can easily be replaced if they become damaged or destroyed; and while they are in use, they have good tone that will travel as far as most bells on the market. Once your bird is fully accustomed to her bells and readily accepts them, you can replace them with better ones – although this is not always possible with certain tail-mounts.

Falconry bells are available in four sizes: small, medium, large and extra large. American bells will cost approximately £12, £15, £18 and £22 respectively, the cheaper variety from Pakistan about £4, £6, £8 and £10 respectively, and the British Titan, in brass, approximately £8.50, £10.50, £13.50 and £15.50 respectively. For those finished in nickel silver and phosphor bronze you should add approximately 25 per cent.

Hawk Baths

An adequate bath is just as essential to the welfare of your bird as any other professionally designed item of equipment. Many beginners try to make a bath from the inside of a plastic dustbin lid, but I would not recommend this. It is much better to buy a bath designed specifically with birds of prey in mind.

Some birds love to bathe and will look forward to a regular soaking, whilst others will give the bath no more than a passing glance. You must never force a reluctant bird into the water. This will only unnerve her more, and possibly turn her off for good. All you can do is allow her the opportunity and hope she eventually takes it.

Bathing is important, as it encourages preening and feather management. Even if you have a stubborn bird who really objects to the bath, you must still offer her the chance over and over again. In the meantime, spray her plumage regularly. Longwings tend to love the water, and very few will not take the plunge. Broadwings and shortwings, however, may be enthusiastic one day but decline the next. Owls can be quite stubborn: they either love it or hate it, there tend to be no in-betweens.

A hawk bath

Baths are generally made of glass fibre, although there are some aluminium ones coming on the market, which I have to say look good, and they may be worth considering. Hawk baths are available in two designs, round or square; either of which is fine, and in small, medium and large sizes. You should make sure you get the correct size for your bird. The bath should be deep enough so that when the hawk dips down into the water, it comes up to or just beyond her shoulders.

You should never leave a bird unsupervised and within reach of the bath for long periods. She may mute (defecate) in the water before going in herself. This is not very hygienic, as she will then be cleaning herself in dirty water, and what is worse, if it is a hot sunny day, she may also drink from it. I would suggest therefore that you do not leave the bath permanently in the weathering unless you are prepared to change the contents very regularly.

There is no need to offer your bird a bath every day, as she may get into the habit of only paddling in the water, instead of using it sensibly. Every two days is sufficient. A Lugger falcon I once had needed to bath prior to being flown. If I did not give her the opportunity, she would fly straight for the nearest puddle. So assess your bird's needs or you may have to spend hours tracking her down. Make sure you never let her bath late in the day, especially during cold weather. If she remains wet and cold overnight she could quite easily catch a chill. Offer her the bath early in the day to allow plenty of drying time.

Never add anything to the bath to help the cleansing. This may seem obvious, but there are people who have mixed soap suds with the water.

Some suppliers will not send baths by mail order as their shape and size makes delivery awkward and expensive. You may therefore have to pick one up personally, or pay extra for the costly post and packaging.

A good large hawk bath will cost approximately £25, and the small and intermediate sizes only slightly cheaper. An aluminium one will cost approximately 10 per cent more.

Leashes

The leash tethers the bird securely to her perch. It is also used as an early training line; she is asked to jump the full length of the extended leash before it is abandoned for the creance. They are generally available in two designs, round or flat. It does not matter what design you use although you may find a round leash makes tying a falconer's knot (see page 64) much easier.

Some birds are annoyingly prone to picking at their leash and undoing it. A red-tailed buzzard I once had was terrible for this. Overnight, she would destroy her leash, and her daily casting always contained strands of fibre. Eventually I used a flat leash and like magic the problem was eradicated.

Leashes

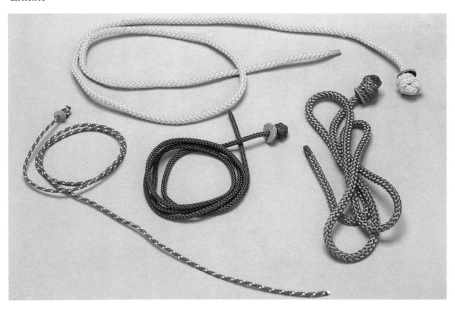

Leashes are available in four sizes: small, medium, large and extra large. The length, the thickness of the cord and the size of the sealed top knot determine the overall size of the finished product. These dimensions will vary slightly from one supplier to another but not to a significant extent. The main thing to take into account when buying one is whether the top knot is adequately tied, heat-sealed, strong and large enough not to fall through the bottom ring of the swivel. The tip of the leash should also be heat-sealed to prevent fraying.

Leashes are made from a variety of materials, and suppliers often disagree over which are best. However, you should never buy a leather one. Leather leashes quickly rot and become brittle. Over the years, many birds have been lost through leather leashes giving in and snapping. Braided Terylene is the best material to my mind. Birds will often mute onto the leash, causing some materials to harden. Terylene remains flexible and resists rotting for far longer than most. Some falconers find that it is too slippery, but this problem is easily overcome by rubbing wax into the fibres, which will also help to keep the second safety knot stable.

Although leashes are inexpensive, you should be able to make your own. When you attend a falconry course you will be shown how to tie and heat-seal the top knot for ultimate safety. You can buy Terylene at a ship's

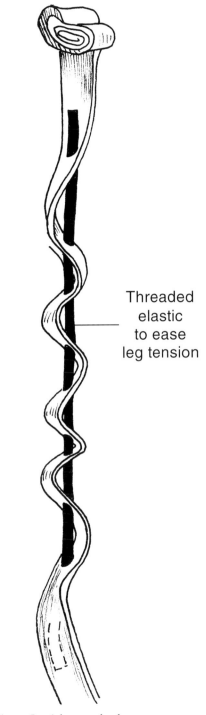

Threaded elastic to ease leg tension

Figure 5   A bumper leash

chandler's and make new leashes as and when you need them.

Terylene is available in many colours. I have never found one particular colour better than another, although I use bright colours as I have a terrible tendency to drop and lose my leashes in the field. A yellow leash, for instance, is far easier to find than one that is dark blue or black.

Bumper leashes (see figure 5) are special leashes which are normally used for shortwings, as they tend to bate fiercely in the early stages of being tethered. They are flat, and have a series of punched holes to accommodate a length of threaded catapult elastic. They are considerably more flexible and far lighter on bating birds' legs than others. The only drawback I find is that they are rather untidy and could become tangled around a perch more easily than the conventional type. Bumper leashes do serve a worthwhile purpose, but I would be reluctant to leave a bird fitted with one unsupervised for long periods.

Another special type of leash is the field or safety leash. This is a very simple alternative to holding a hawk by her jesses alone whilst out in the field. A small hole is punched towards the bottom of each flying jess and a length of creance cord threaded through. This is then tied by means of a falconer's knot to the D-ring of the glove. However, although the knot can be untied quickly, I find it a burden when a slip at quarry is spontaneous.

I am often surprised by the number of falconers, from beginners through to intermediate participants, who are unable to tie a falconer's knot. Granny knots etc. are just not good enough for leashes, and certainly no substitute for a well-heeled falconer's knot. Its design is very well suited to falconry, as it can be tied and untied with one hand whilst the bird is sitting astute on the glove. Although it was not designed exclusively for tethering birds of prey, it has proven ideal for this purpose, as it is quick, safe and strong.

It is imperative that you tie

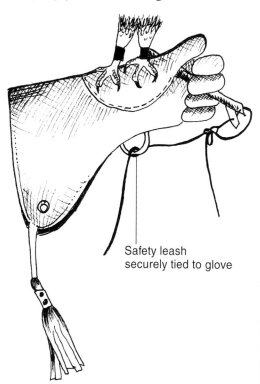

Safety leash
securely tied to glove

Figure 6   A field safety leash

this knot speedily and efficiently. You must practise constantly until you are able to do it blindfolded, as during the hawking season you will be leaving home early and returning late, often in pitch darkness.

There are several ways to tie the falconer's knot, and you should do it in the way best suited to you. Providing the end result is acceptable, it does not matter how you get there.

The instructions that follow, and the picture sequence, therefore describe the procedure with the bird on the left hand.

1. With an imaginary bird sitting on your left hand, guide the tip of the leash through the tethering ring. Place it in between your index and second fingers, laying the remainder over your third and fourth fingers.
2. Swing your right hand under the knotted section of leash until it comes to rest between your thumb and index finger.
3. Place your thumb under the knotted end of the leash and pull back; do not move the rest of your hand.
4. Keeping your thumb exactly where it is, swing your palm underneath the knotted section of the leash and up to meet your thumb, guiding the loop into the loop which is being held by your thumb.
5. Using your thumb and second finger, guide the loop through by approximately one inch.
6. Guide the knot towards the tethering ring by pulling with your left hand.
7. Pass the tip end of the leash through the loop and lay both sections of the leash neatly side by side.
8. For maximum safety, tie a second knot in exactly the same way.

To release the knot, simply pull the tip end of the leash out from the loop and pull.

Whenever a bird is tethered to her perch, she must be sitting relaxed upon the fist. This way you have total control of any sudden movements or bating. Likewise, when you take the bird from the perch, you must first step her onto your fist before undoing the knot.

If the bird bates when you are midway through tethering her to the perch, stop immediately and aid her carefully back onto your fist. This will eliminate the possibility of feather damage.

Providing you have tied both knots efficiently, there will be no need to add two or three extra granny knots. This will only make the leash appear untidy and serves no constructive purpose.

You should practise tying the leash to your falconry glove; this is quite a tricky exercise but will easily be achieved after repeated attempts.

To keep the leash supple and manageable, clean away dried mud

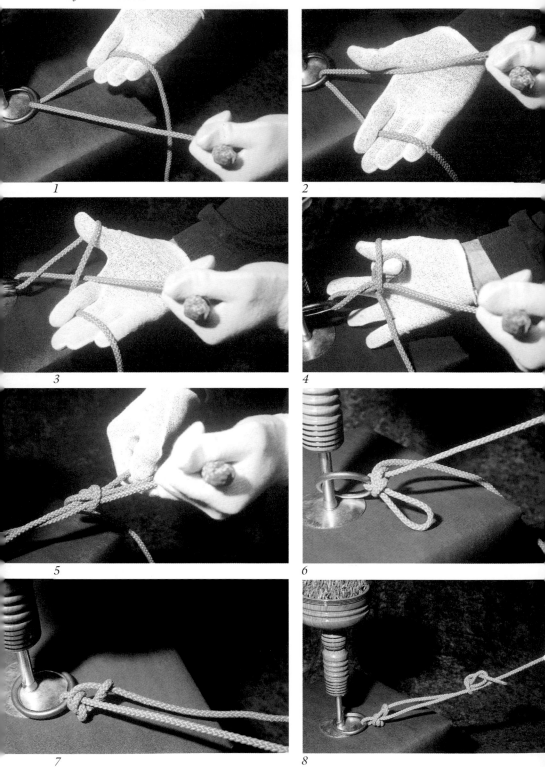

1

2

3

4

5

6

7

8

and faeces, as a hard leash will be an unmanageable leash.

As well as tying the knot, you must also think about correct leash lengths. The length is correct if there is adequate leash from the swivel to the tethering ring once the bird has been seated to her perch. With a good length the leash will be just long enough to allow the tethering ring to sit comfortably upon the ground, with approximately 2–3 inches of slack. Never allow too much slack, as the bird is then able to gather speed when bating, which could severely damage her legs.

A round leash will cost approximately £2 for the small size, £2.50 for medium, £3 for large and £3.50 for extra large. Flat leashes will be slightly dearer. Very few suppliers stock bumper leashes, so you may have to design one yourself. However, no beginner should contemplate buying an *Accipiter* for his first bird, and bumper leashes are designed primarily for these birds. Field leashes are not sold by suppliers as they are only a length of creance cord.

Scales

Scales are without doubt the most important item of equipment you will be buying, so ensure that you get good ones. They are critical to the welfare of all birds of prey and owls that are intended to be flown free. Once you have gained considerable knowledge and expertise in controlling a bird's weight, the scales may become just a back-up to confirm your visual and physical assessment of your bird's condition. Until then, they are the key to your bird's continuing welfare.

Old fashioned scales like the spring-loaded kitchen type should never be used. If they constantly register different weights, they could be the cause of your bird's death. So be certain that the ones you use are reliable and carry a good

Digital scales

manufacturer's name.

I recommend digital scales rather than the large, bulky balance type. Most digital scales will weigh up to, and beyond 4 pounds, which is quite adequate for the vast majority of birds suitable for the beginner. If you have a heavier bird than this, such as a European eagle-owl, then you will probably have no alternative but to purchase the balance type with a selection of loose weights. But the advantage of digital scales is that they are light, easily transported and compact.

Before you weigh your bird, you must check that the scales are reading accurately. The easiest way to do this is to purchase either a 2-ounce or 3-ounce fishing weight and weigh it. If the weight registers correctly, then the scales are suitable. But never weigh a bird without first checking for accuracy.

Whatever type of scales you buy, they will have to be converted to accommodate a bird. She will require a good comfortable sitting point whilst you take a reading, and a T-perch built onto the base of the scales is ideal. When the bird is sitting on the T-perch, make absolutely sure that no part of her plumage is touching either the scales or the perch itself, as this could give you a false reading. Give her plenty of space, making sure that there is nothing within her reach. Be absolutely sure that she is sitting motionless before you take the reading. I remember once seeing a falconer weighing his bird whilst she was rotating on the T-perch. Any recording he took was bound to be incorrect.

Materials for a T-perch

- Two lengths of 6in yard-broom handle (thick diameter)
- One 3in x 3in x 1in wooden plate
- Astroturf or leather
- Strong glue or industrial double-sided adhesive tape

To construct your T-perch, follow these instructions:

1. Drill a hole, slightly wider than the broom handle, just over halfway into the wooden plate.
2. Drill a hole, also slightly wider than the broom handle, in the centre of one piece of the handle.
3. Glue one end of the undrilled piece of handle vertically into the hole in the plate and the other end into the hole in the second piece of handle.
4. Fix the plate securely to the scales either with glue or with double-sided tape covering the cross-section with either Astroturf or leather.

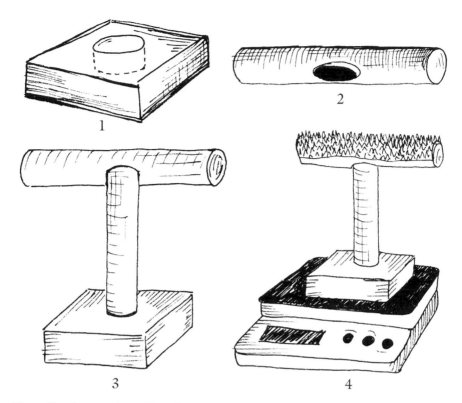

Figure 7   Constructing a T-perch

These measurements are acceptable for most birds, but if you feel they are not quite right, adjust them accordingly.

Digital scales can be purchased from household stores for approximately £25. Ready-made perches are very expensive, but making one as described above is very easy and will cost you virtually nothing.

Radio Telemetry

A radio telemetry system will be your single most expensive item of equipment if you decide to buy one. But falconers have different opinions about its usefulness. Those who fly Harris hawks, red-tails, buzzards or owls often do not bother with telemetry, as they believe their birds will never become lost, whilst those who fly goshawks and falcons will not fly without it.

A telemetry system consists of a receiver box, a transmitter and an antenna. The bird carries the transmitter, which is often referred to as a tag. Tags are available in different stages. Stage one is small and

A radio telemetry system

lightweight, and is ideal for small birds such as merlins and kestrels. The larger and heavier stage two has a longer range, and is fine for hawks and bigger owls. The stage three tag is the biggest and heaviest of all, but it does have the furthest range. It is primarily used for longwings, but can also be used for hawks and larger owls.

Tags are attached to the bird around the leg, the tail or the neck, although neck tagging is mainly reserved for longwings. Personally I use a tail mount (see pages 80-1), a simple device fastened to the bird's two centre deck feathers which is designed to accommodate the tag securely. Placing a tag on a bird's leg is too untidy for me, and it could easily entangle a hawk whilst she is sitting in a tree. As for neck-tagging, I hate the thought of anything fixed around a bird's neck.

There are now many suppliers selling telemetry systems, and the market is becoming saturated with new designs each year. The majority of units I have field tested have fallen below the standard I feel is necessary to locate a lost bird with reasonable ease. Some are too complicated to use, whilst others have given a strong signal at long range but are weak at pinpointing the exact location of a bird when it is at close quarters. Whatever system you choose, it needs to be reliable, with a quick repair system in case it develops a fault in mid-season – a system that has to be shipped across Europe for repair is no good to you. It should also be easy to use and light to carry.

The design must allow for quick assembly, but above all, it should be competitively priced. Before parting with any money, you must field test all the systems that are within your budget; never order over the telephone from the information given in a catalogue alone.

I am often asked by students attending our falconry courses whether radio telemetry is really necessary. All I can say is, no, providing you do not lose your bird. But if you envisage attending field meets throughout the season, which will probably entail driving great distances, then telemetry is a must. If you lost your bird miles away from where you live it would be impractical to go home when it became dark and return at first light, whereas with a telemetry system you would stand a realistic chance of finding your bird before darkness falls. You would have to be very lucky to find a bird on your

A falcon fitted with a tag

own in the countryside, but a good system will narrow the range down and you should maintain a signal reading throughout your search. Personally I would never fly any of my birds without one. Of course, the greatest telemetry system in the world cannot guarantee the safe return of a lost bird. It is not a magic wand, but it will help tremendously. Never be fooled into purchasing systems that are extremely cheap – they are probably not very good. If you can, get one during the close season so that you have a few months to familiarise yourself with its workings. A good system will cost approximately £500–£600 for the receiver and antenna. Stage one tags cost approximately £70, stage two £90 and stage three £110.

Lamping and Lamping Equipment

Lamping is a form of hawking which is done at night with the aid of a strong beam of light. The lamp is switched on to illuminate the eyes of unsuspecting quarry, and the bird flies it by following the direction of light. Although lamping for rabbit can be extremely exciting, it has certain risks. Your bird will be flying free with only a beam of light to aid its vision. There is therefore far more chance of losing her, as raptors' eyesight is no better than that of humans at night.

Lamping is a good proposition for the falconer who has limited opportunities of mid-week flying. Before you set off for an evening's hawking, however, you should alert the local police station and explain what you are doing. Then when they receive phone calls from worried residents and motorists, they will be able to tell them exactly what is going on. If the police have to come out to investigate, it is a waste of their time. If you have obtained prior permission from the landowner, as you should, he or she will no doubt alert surrounding farms. If there are roads or lanes within reach of the lamp's beam, you should be extremely careful not to blind passing drivers. Common sense is a must when hawking in this way.

To be successful you must have help. Although modern lamps are quite light and compact, it is still impossible to slip your bird off one hand and keep control of the lamp in the other.

A bird that has always flown and hunted by day cannot suddenly be asked to fly at night; you will certainly lose her if you do. She must be trained at night in just the same way as during the day. If you attend a falconry course, you should ask the instructor about the methods you need to use. And radio telemetry is essential when lamping.

Rabbits can become what is called lamp-shy when particular land is often used by lampers, and bolt straight for cover as soon as the lamp is switched on. To overcome this, you can attach a red or green filter over the standard white beam; this often fools the quarry.

The market is full of makes and designs of night-vision aid. Although most seem to be adequate, the one I would recommend is the Clulite. It is a lightweight, compact system that is very competitively priced, and over the years it has proved itself to be very reliable. Dedicated attachments such as car battery chargers, coloured filters etc. are easily available, which makes this lamp one of the best buys.

A basic lamp kit comprises a battery pack, a charger and a lamp. Prices will vary considerably from one make to another, but £80–100 is about the right figure for something well made and reliable. Attachments will obviously be classed as extras.

Cadges

There are two types of cadge, the travelling cadge and the field cadge. As their name suggests, travelling cadges are used to accommodate birds whilst they are in transit. Some people may say that this is an unnecessary expense as the bird could simply sit on an indoor perch. This is true, to a certain extent, but the design of a travelling cadge makes it far more comfortable if the roads are bumpy. Travelling cadges are much heavier than large indoor perches, and they are steadier when placed in the back of a vehicle as they are much wider.

This is the way I transport the majority of my birds to shows and field meets, and I believe it helps to protect their feathers from damage. Providing the tail feathers do not trail in mutes or touch the inside of the cadge or the base of the vehicle, I am sure the bird is happier to travel this way. If the section where the bird sits is wide and padded in thick carpet or Astroturf, then this is probably the best means of transportation.

Owls, however, present more of a problem as they cannot be hooded. Unless you have an exceptionally steady bird which never thrashes around whilst being transported, you will have to transport her by a different means. A well-designed travelling box is the obvious choice.

If you want to transport a number of birds on a cadge, remember that one could easily lose her footing and knock another bird from her section, causing an ugly scene. Add a second internal mirror to your windscreen so that you can keep an eye on the birds' activities at all times.

You should make sure that there are no fumes circulating inside the vehicle. Never carry a petrol can, even if it is empty, as its fumes will have a devastating effect on your birds; likewise will tins of paint etc., that do not have their lids firmly fixed.

Before transporting any bird you should first find out whether

Lamping equipment

A travelling cadge

additional insurance cover is required. If you were to have an accident your standard cover might not be adequate, and you could be in serious trouble if you were stopped by the police.

Field cadges (see figure 8) are very rarely seen these days, except on big longwing field meets. They are designed to carry about four falcons into the field at the same time. Although similar in design to the travelling cadge, the field cadge should be made as light and comfortable for the carrier as possible. The inner panel of the field cadge is abandoned so the falconer (or cadger as he is often called) can step within the frame, and pull the straps over his shoulders. Field

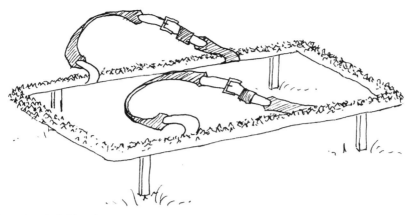

Figure 8   A field cadge

cadges are used solely for longwings, as they are the only birds taken into the field in any numbers. The birds are then flown individually or in casts once or twice, before being rehooded.

Cadges are quite expensive to buy – the post and packaging alone will be extremely high. A well-made cadge will cost approximately £100 but very few suppliers stock them so you may have difficulty ordering one. Alternatively you could ask your supplier about correct measurements and materials and make one for yourself.

Travelling Boxes

A travelling box is ideal for birds that are hood-shy. It must have adequate ventilation holes, which should be situated towards the bottom, thus preventing the bird from looking out and allowing only minimal light to enter. It must be spacious enough, particularly around the head, tail and wings, to allow the bird to turn around completely with ease. If she is in any way restricted, she may feel stressed and this could result in her thrashing about, which is something that must be prevented at all costs. An adequate perch should be fitted;

A travelling box

it should be thick and covered with a suitable gripping surface, such as Astroturf or thick carpet. Avoid anything which is slippery, such as bare varnished wood or certain leathers.

An eyass of the year will not sit on a normal outdoor perch – she will not even sit upon the fist. You cannot therefore expect her to sit calmly on a perch in a travelling box when you first collect her from the breeders. You will therefore have to find another method of transporting her (see page 85).

I said in the previous section that I transport my birds to field meets and shows hooded on a travelling cadge. When I go home, however, I often use a travelling box instead. I never hood a bird if she has eaten prior to a journey, no matter how small the meal may have been. If she becomes a little travel sick she could quite easily be restricted from vomiting by the hood, which might even result in her choking. A travelling box is therefore a far safer proposition.

I also mentioned that because they cannot be hooded, owls will probably need to be transported in a travelling box. Larger species will need a specially constructed box, but for smaller owls I have found that the cardboard boxes which are sold for transporting cats are suitable, if you line the bottom with an old bath towel to cushion the bird's feathers. Try to buy corrugated boxes as they keep their shape better and last longer. They are available from good pet shops or veterinary surgeries.

Travelling boxes must be kept spotlessly clean. A quick application of a solution of diluted sterilising fluid after each use should be adequate. Lay a section of carpet on the bottom, but do not fix it down. You will then be able to extract it at liberty, and give it a good brush-down. Try not to use anything that will rustle, like newspaper, as this could unnerve the bird.

If you carry your bird on your left hand, the door of the box should open to the right. This puts you in the correct position to step the bird onto the perch and close the door with the ungloved hand. There should be a small hole in the bottom left-hand corner of the door to allow you to thread the leash tip through and tie two granny knots. This means you can take hold of the leash before opening the door and you will not be taken unawares by any sudden movements. But do make sure the bird always has an adequate length of leash inside to enable her to move freely.

Hopefully your bird will remain quiet and relaxed until the end of your journey. However, a quiet bird might just possibly be a dead or dying bird, so make regular safety checks. Moreover, when driving you should try to make the journey as comfortable as possible for the bird. Never speed, swerve or brake suddenly, as this could cause the box to topple over. Always give yourself plenty of time to get to a venue and drive with thought and care.

A suitable travelling box made from marine plywood will cost approximately £80. Very few suppliers stock them for mail order, however, so you may have to enquire once again with your equipment supplier about adequate sizes, materials and designs, and construct one yourself.

Anklets

Aylmeri anklets are leather bracelets that are firmly fixed around a bird's tarsus so that jesses can be fitted. There is a variety of leathers that can be used, but like many falconers, I find kangaroo hide by far the best. It is immensely strong yet supple. Its suitability is, however, reflected in its price; it is extremely expensive, and often quite difficult to obtain. Nevertheless its ability to remain manageable for lengthy periods alone justifies its high price.

Kangaroo hide is available in various colours, although black and tan are the most common. It is generally sold by the square foot, which is an expensive way to buy it. You will be given the choice of three thicknesses: fine, medium and heavy grade. It is important that you use the correct grade, as different species need different strengths and weights of leather. If it is too weak, it will tear. However, make sure you do not unbalance your bird by using a heavy leather when it is not necessary. If in doubt, ask the supplier what he or she recommends. Whatever leather you choose to use, the most important thing to remember is to test it for strength and avoid anything that you are able to tear easily with your hands.

To make and attach Aylmeri anklets you will need: leather, a leather punch, a closing tool, brass eyelets, a scalpel or leather-cutting knife, sharp scissors and grease. Then follow these instructions (see also figure 9):

1. Cut a strip of leather 8cm long. The width will depend on the species of bird and size of brass eyelet to be used. As a general guide, it should be approximately 1–2cm for longwings, broadwings and small to medium-sized owls, and approximately 3–4cm for shortwings and larger owls.
2. Place the anklet around the bird's leg to check exactly where the eyelet holes will need to be punched.
3. Punch out the eyelet holes and make tiny nicks along the anklet both top and bottom to make it more flexible. Grease it thoroughly and allow the grease to penetrate.
4. Once again place the anklet around the bird's leg to double check for a correct fit before closing it firmly into place using the closing tool and brass eyelet, making sure not to twist the leather.

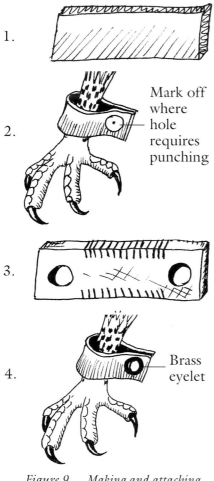

1.

2. Mark off where hole requires punching

3.

4. Brass eyelet

Figure 9   Making and attaching Aylmeri anklets

5. Once the anklet is attached, trim off all surplus leather around the eyelet with scissors to aid appearance.

When you are using sharp scissors close to a bird, be extra cautious. I have known people injure birds with scissors through carelessness. Always make sure the bird is comfortable and settled before you use such implements.

The anklet must be a perfect fit – it should slide with ease up and down the leg. If it is too large the bird may step out of it altogether; if it is too small, you will inflict unnecessary pain. You should keep changing it until you are quite happy with it.

Note that Aylmeri anklets must be fitted below any identity ring or bewit.

Anklets do not cost very much to buy, but different species of bird have widely differing leg sizes. I would therefore recommend that you make them yourself, so that you can make sure that they are just right for your bird.

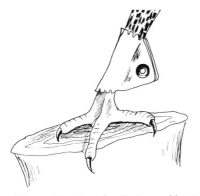

Figure 10   A wider-fitting anklet for shortwings and large owls

Jesses

Jesses are leather straps which serve the same purpose as a dog lead; they give you something to hold onto your bird with. Once again, kangaroo is the finest leather available for making them.

There are two types of jess currently in use: the traditional type and the modern button variety. A traditional jess consists of one piece of leather which is placed around a bird's leg and folded through a series of prepared slits. However, the slit which accommodates the swivel could easily cause a bird to become snarled if it is pitched ie when the bird is resting in a tree, so traditional jesses should never be used on owls, hawks or buzzards, but only on longwings, as they are trained not to pitch in trees.

Although traditional jesses look nice and neat when attached, I find that they are a lot of trouble when they need replacing, as help is needed to cast the bird. Button jesses with Aylmeri anklets are far easier, as one can change the jesses regularly without having to cast the bird. There are two types available: the mews jess and the flying jess.

Mews jesses have small incisions which allow a swivel to be threaded through. Because of these incisions, you must never allow a bird to fly free with mews jesses. Some falconers wet and twist the ends, or apply an electric cable-tie to turn a mews jess temporarily into a safer flying jess. This is wrong, and you should never do it. You should use custom-made flying jesses whenever your bird is in free flight. Flying jesses have no slits, although some may have a small hole punched towards the tip end to accommodate a safety leash, which should cause no danger whilst a bird is sitting in a tree.

Jesses should be greased regularly and changed frequently throughout the season. Spare jesses must always be carried in the field.

To make jesses you will need leather, a leather punch, a scalpel or leather knife, grease, a metal ruler and long-pointed pliers or forceps. Then follow the instructions below (see also figure 11).

1. Cut a strip of leather a little wider than the brass eyelet for which the jess is intended. The length depends on the size of perch you are using; ask your supplier what length is recommended when you buy the perch.

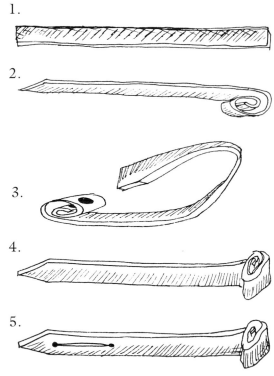

Figure 11   Making and attaching mews jesses

2. Cut one end into a gradual v-shape and fold the other twice to form a button.
3. Using one of the larger holes on the punch, punch a hole through the three layers of leather. Aim the pointed end of the jess into the button and pull it through using forceps or long-pointed pliers.
4. Pull the point completely through until it is taut. You now have a raw jess.
5. Towards the end of the jess, punch two small holes and cut a slit. The size of the slit depends on the size of the swivel to be used. Grease it and allow the grease to penetrate.

Like anklets, jesses are very inexpensive to buy from falconry suppliers, but because of differences in leg size, it is better to make them yourself.

It is important that you keep your jesses well maintained. If they are hard, you will not be able to attach them to the swivel.

The swivel is fixed to the jesses with one hand. This is probably the hardest job for a beginner, and initially you may think it is impossible. But if you practise constantly, you will get the knack. Just follow the instructions below and refer to figure 12.

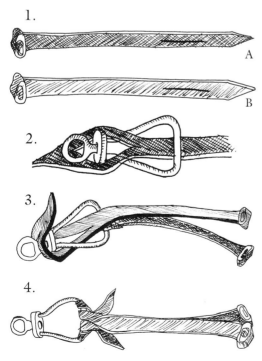

Figure 12 Attaching the swivel

1. Cut and prepare the jesses as described, and apply a good wax to penetrate the pores of the leather.
2. Place jess A through the top ring of the swivel and over the bottom ring. Position it in the right place towards the top of the swivel and pull it taut.
3. Place jess B through the top ring of the swivel but this time from the opposite direction. Again position it correctly and pull it taut.
4. Jesses should be neat and tidy on the swivel, and made in such a way that their size appears correct in relation to the size of the swivel. This will avoid restriction of the swivel turning.

Bewits

Bewits are fine leather straps for attaching hawking bells to a bird's leg. There are three types: the traditional bewit, the cable-tie bewit with the cable-tie firmly sealed in a plastic sleeve, and the button bewit. Personally, I use the button bewit as I can simply take it off the leg to change the bell or to add additional grease. With a traditional bewit I would have to cut it off.

To make a button bewit you will need the following items of equipment: leather, a scalpel or leather knife, a leather punch, a metal ruler, long-nose pliers or forceps and grease. Then follow these instructions (see also figure 13).

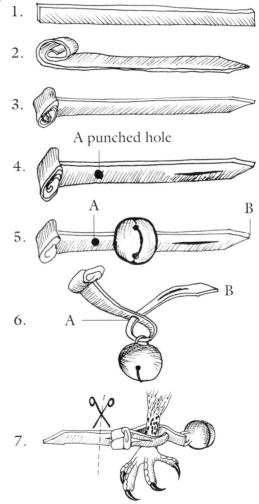

1. Cut a section of leather approximately 14 cm long and as wide as the bewit clip or keeper on the bell. Grease it well, and allow the grease to penetrate.
2. Cut one end of the leather so that it tapers to a point, and fold the opposite end once to form a button.
3. Punch a smallish hole through the button and make a raw button bewit in exactly the same way as you would a raw jess (see pages 76-8).
4. Punch a small hole, approximately 2.5 cm from the bottom of the button; the size will vary from bird to bird, as all legs are different. About 5.5 cm down from the button, cut a slit approximately 1 cm long.
5. Slide the bell onto the bewit just below the punched hole at point A.
6. Place point B through point A.

Figure 13   Making and attaching leather bell bewits

7. Place the bewit around the bird's leg, with the button through the slit. Trim off all surplus leather to finish and enhance the appearance.

The more bewits you make the better they will become. Persevere until you achieve the perfect size for your bird.

Tail Mounts

If you prefer to tail-bell your bird rather than leg-bell her, you will need a tail mount. Tail mounts are attached in one of two ways. The ones supplied by Eagle-Owl are designed to be fixed to both centre deck feathers and hold both the bell and a telemetry transmitter. The other method is to use a piece of leather which is fixed onto one centre deck thus leaving the other free to accommodate the transmitter. The brass mount that holds the transmitter will have to be purchased from a supplier. Although this method is satisfactory, I much prefer tail mounts which are firmly attached to both deck feathers.

To make and attach a tail mount you will need a 2cm wide by 3cm long guitar plectrum, leather, a leather punch, superglue, talcum powder, a piece of thick paper for isolating the feathers, pre-waxed thread, a curved needle and sharp scissors. The method is as follows (see also figure 14):

1. Punch two small holes A and B, left and right at the top of the plectrum.
2. Cut a strip of leather approximately 10cm long, and as wide as the holes, tapering one end into a gradual point.
3. Thread the tapered end of the leather through hole A of the plectrum. Slide the bell onto it, before threading it through hole B. Glue the leather between points A and B so that both the leather and the bell are held firmly against the plectrum. Cut the ends of the leather to an adequate length, approximately 5mm.
4. Isolate the centre deck feathers with thick paper.
5. Glue one piece of leather to one feather, keeping up a firm pressure until it has bonded before doing the same to the other strip. Cut two lengths of pre-waxed thread and tie them firmly around each feather for total security.
    Once the tail mount is in place, douse it with talcum powder and blow away the excess, making sure not to get it in the bird's eyes, mouth or nostrils.

When fixing the tail mount you will need the help of someone who has a little experience in casting and holding down a bird of prey.

Whenever you cast a bird it must be for as short a period as possible so as not to upset her any more than is absolutely necessary. You should use a large, soft, bath towel to hold her steady so that there is no risk of feather damage. Place the bird on a cushion so she has something to grip and something to lie upon.

Tail mounts are fixed permanently and should only come off annually when the bird moults her feathers. You should therefore ask an experienced falconer to guide you through the motions to make sure you get it right as you only get the one chance. Fixing a tail mount is something you will be shown how to do on a good falconry course.

Sundries

When looking through suppliers' catalogues, you will notice that some have a section entitled 'Sundries'. Strictly speaking, these are not actually falconry equipment but tools and accessories, or items intended to help you maintain your bird. They are all necessary pieces of equipment, with their own important roles.

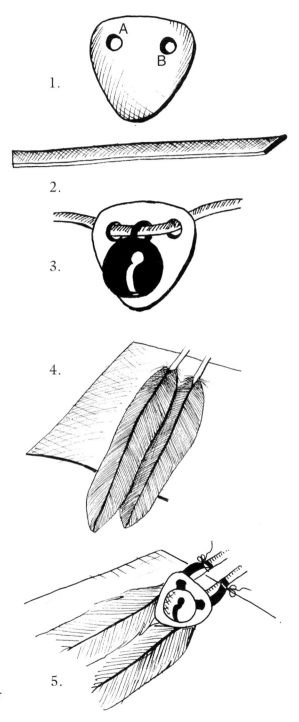

Figure 14 Making and attaching a tail mount

Brass Eyelets

Brass eyelets are washers that close the leather Aylmeri anklets or bracelets which go around a bird of prey's leg (see pages 75-6) and allow jesses to be inserted. They are also embossed onto falconry bags or flying waistcoats for safe storage of spare jesses. They are very similar to the eyelets in shoes, through which shoelaces go, although footwear eyelets are often plastic-coated. There are two parts to the eyelet: the main holding section and the backing washer.

Eyelets are available in small, medium, large and extra large sizes, each designed for different widths and thicknesses of anklet, and for different degrees of strength. The size of the eyelet also determines the overall thickness and width of jess that can be inserted.

Eyelets normally come in packets of 20, and cost approximately £1.50 for the small size, £2 for medium, £2.50 for large and £3 for extra large.

Closing Tools

Closing tools are for fixing the Aylmeri anklets; there is no standard substitute. They are available in four sizes: small, medium, large and extra large. The small size looks very much like standard pliers, but the others are slightly different. They comprise two separate pieces of metal. One section holds the backing washer of the brass eyelet and the other the main section. They are placed into the eyelet holes and screwed or crimped together, thus tightening the anklets firmly together.

It is important that you buy top-quality closing tools as the cheaper variety tend to bend and snap when pressure is applied. They will cost approximately £5 for the small size, £7.50 for medium, £12.50 for large and £17 for extra large.

Leather Punches

A leather punch is a valuable item of equipment, which you will need for making holes in anklets and jesses, and for making a flat leash. Most come with a rotating head that gives you six sizes of hole.

A quality leather punch will cost approximately £10.

Feather Straighteners

A feather straightener is another valuable item of equipment. It is a brass tong which you heat over a boiling kettle and then pull down along the bird's feathers to iron away bent and untidy feathers. Feathers that are out of shape make a bird look terribly messy, and with this simple device there is now never any need for it.

A brass feather straightener will cost approximately £10.

Whistles
When choosing a whistle you only need to worry about one thing: that your bird can hear you. As long as that is the case, anything will do. Indeed, if you can whistle loudly enough naturally, while running at the same time, you need not buy a whistle at all.

Many falconers use a standard referee's whistle, and that is fine for recalling a bird to the fist. Personally, I prefer not to use this kind as it reminds me too much of a football or rugby match. A shepherd's whistle has a very good tone, but it is difficult to master and needs a lot of practice. Try to test an assortment of whistles at a game fair until you come across one that you are happy with.

Most standard whistles cost approximately £2.50.

Grease
Grease is invaluable for the maintenance of jesses, anklets and gloves. Leather soon becomes dry, but that does not mean it is useless. A regular greasing will revive it, and bring back its suppleness. On many occasions I have seen falconers battling to attach stiff, inflexible jesses to the swivel, to no avail. So ask your supplier which variety is most suitable, and make sure you have a tin handy at all times.

A 5ml tin will cost approximately £3.50 and probably last a whole season.

Needle Files and Clippers
Although I do not normally believe that a novice should skimp when buying equipment and accessories, this does not necessarily apply to needle files. You will pay a lot for a set of needle files from a supplier, because they are generally of exceptional quality and come complete with a leather wallet. But a standard pack of needle files from a tool shop will do the job just as well.

Needle files are a must for coping beaks and attending to talons. A pack of six will contain all the shapes you need. You will also need clippers, which can be purchased from all good pet shops.

No beginner should *ever* attempt to cope a beak or cut talons until he has been shown how to do it by a professional. Even then he should ensure that an experienced falconer is present while he does it until he is confident of his ability.

Files bought from a tool shop will cost approximately £2.50. From a falconry supplier they will cost upwards of £17. You will also need good-quality clippers, which cost around £5.

A student with her first bird

CHAPTER FOUR

Buying Your First Bird

Of all the thrills that you are likely to encounter in your falconry career, one of the greatest will be the journey to pick up your very first bird. I know I shall never forget my own.

You will have attended a falconry course, perhaps joined a club, constructed a weathering and bought all the necessary equipment. At last you can meet your bird, which will probably have been ordered many months before. After all your intensive work, the time you have spent learning and the considerable financial outlay you have so far incurred, it is important that you are not disappointed by finding that you have bought a bird which may be carrying any kind of defect.

Although most breeders are honourable people with high standards, I would recommend you to take someone along with you who has adequate experience and the ability to give your prospective bird a thorough going-over. If you placed an order for a female Harris hawk, that is obviously what you should get, not a male and certainly not a common buzzard. But it could happen; an inexperienced beginner would not necessarily know the difference.

Obviously you will need something in which to transport your bird home. You should therefore go armed with a suitably sized cardboard box containing a soft towel. Not all breeders will supply you with one, and most will not even mention it during any correspondence as they will take it for granted that you will bring one.

Checking Your Bird

Very few breeders will allow you to see the bird in the aviary, so you will be asked to wait whilst your bird is caught up. Do not be suspicious about this – it now seems to be common practice. Once it has been caught up, however, it should be made available for examination. Do not allow the breeder to place it directly into the box. It is understandable for beginners to feel shy about asking questions of someone who is probably well known and well respected, and who has a reputation for producing excellent young. Do not be put off, however. If the breeder's reputation is justified, then he should go out of his way to help you with your questions, understanding that your knowledge is limited.

Your assessment should begin from the moment the bird is brought inside. A parent-reared bird will be extremely nervous and do everything in her power to break free given the opportunity. She will not welcome the unfamiliar environment and may make her feelings known vocally. Her breathing could be heavy; this is quite common, and not a sign of illness. If, on the other hand, she is relaxed and takes everything in her stride, this should give you cause for suspicion, as it is more the behaviour of an imprinted bird who is familiar to humans and a human environment.

First assess the bird's feet; they should be clean, and show no signs of scabbing, redness or swelling. The legs should also be clean and undamaged. Check that the bird has a tight grip by putting on a gauntlet and placing it into the talons. Look closely at both wings and make sure they open and close smoothly, with no abrasions to the under-parts. The eyes should be large and bright, and the nares (nostrils) must have no signs of discharge, as this could mean she has a chill. Make sure her beak is not chipped or broken, and that there is no damage to the cere. Try and smell her breath, which should not be foul. Look closely at each feather to see that none are bent, broken or missing.

If you are happy and decide to buy the bird, take another close look at the talons. If they are overgrown, they should be clipped back before placing her into the box ready for the journey home. If it is a hot day, try to keep the box out of direct sunlight as this will only add to the stress which the bird has already suffered. Although you must never drive erratically or dangerously, you should try to get the bird home as quickly as possible, without stopping for lunch or refreshments. Remember that from the moment your bird was caught up, her lifestyle has changed, and will continue to do so. From that moment on, everything will be new to her. You should therefore ensure that she is not upset or stressed any more than is absolutely necessary.

Settling Your Bird In

When you reach your destination, everything should have been prepared for her arrival – the leather for cutting out the anklets, the punch, the eyelets, the scalpel etc. The jesses could have been made in advance, as their length and size will not be totally dependent on the bird's specific leg size in the same way as anklets.

You will almost certainly not be able to retrieve the bird from the box, cast her and attach the anklets etc. alone, and you should not even try. Enlist the help of a competent friend with a good-sized towel. Gently open the box, and get your friend to take hold of the bird, cast her in the towel and lay her on her back. If you keep her head covered you will find that she will remain fairly still. Place the anklet leather around a leg and mark the size. Cut and prepare the anklet and fix it carefully, making sure not to twist the leather as it is sealed together. Once this is done, thread the jess through. Do the same to the other leg, but this time fit the swivel and leash whilst the bird is in the cast position. Put on your falconry glove and release her from the towel. As soon as you have guided her onto the fist she will immediately hang upside down; this is quite normal. My advice is to then put her inside the weathering to calm down.

It is important that your hawk is monitored at regular intervals until she has relaxed and found her feet.

Suitable Birds for Beginners

The modern-day falconer has a vast selection of birds to choose from. It is impossible to describe every variety, and in any case very few species make viable birds for beginners. Some are not easily available, others cost too much, many are physically inadequate and a great number have very delicate metabolisms which are too complicated for the beginner to deal with.

At the Eagle-Owl School of Falconry, we recommend a choice of three hawks and two owls for beginners. We suggest that they do not start with falcons; we believe that these are birds to progress on to. The golden rule to remember is: the smaller a bird's physical stature the harder it will be to attain a flying weight without killing her. A beginner should therefore not consider smaller birds such as kestrels or barn owls, where the margin of error between life and death is extremely delicate. Your first bird should therefore be hardy and versatile, allowing you greater flexibility. Of course this does not mean you can continually get the weight control wrong, as even the largest birds are somewhat delicate in this respect.

The Common Buzzard (Buteo buteo)
We often hear that the buzzard makes an ideal beginner's bird, but I do not entirely agree. Although it is of a healthy size, it is all too often subject to inconsistent temperament swings, which can be spontaneous and nasty. Buzzards are often lazy and slow in flight, and the vast majority struggle to develop the demanding skills that are required for success in the field. Their feet are relatively small in comparison with their overall frame, so they are easily thrown off rabbits. The females, although slower off the fist, are a third larger than the males, and will find it easier to bind themselves to quarry.

Training a buzzard takes about the same length of time as most other hawks, but the end result will not be as good. A novice who buys a buzzard will soon want to move onto something with more

A common buzzard

ability, and this often means that the bird is sold or becomes stagnant within the aviary. They need to be handled and flown hard every day to maintain their fitness and to keep them alert.

Males cost approximately £200 and females approximately £300.

The Red-tailed Buzzard (Buteo jamaicensis)

The red-tail has a reputation for being aggressive, lazy and not suited to a beginner. I have to disagree with all of this assessment, as I have found them to be acceptably mannered, eager to kill and incredibly brave whilst in the field. They are excellent from trees and obedient, and they will work well over a dog. It is vitally important that they should be fully parent-reared, however; if not, they will be extremely aggressive and potentially dangerous to the falconer.

Red-tails can be trained at a good pace, but it is important to get the bird on an early kill. They will need to be handled every day and flown as much as possible to maintain and maximise their fitness and to keep their temperament in check; they can revert to being wild extremely quickly.

In summary, the red-tail is a good beginner's bird because of its size and ability in the field. Males tend to have the better temperament and are faster off the fist than the larger females. However, because of their natural strength, I would not recommend a bird of this kind for a juvenile.

Males will cost approximately £250, and females up to £400.

A red-tailed buzzard

The Harris Hawk (Parabuteo unicintus)

Probably the most used hawking bird in the world, the Harris hawk is an extremely social bird with a very easy-going temperament. Both the male and female are a good proposition, having healthy-sized feet. Either used off the fist or via trees, the Harris will achieve success time after time in the field. I class it as a weekender's bird, as it will remain relaxed throughout the week and be ready and willing for hunting at the weekend, although full fitness will not come this way.

Harris hawks bring the added attraction of flying in pairs, just as they would do in the wild. The smaller male leads the chase, knowing that the larger female will be at close quarters ready to lend a helping hand if necessary. Their only shortcoming is their reluctance to work over dogs, as in the wild their main predator is the coyote.

In summary, the Harris hawk is an excellent beginner's bird, and one ideally suited to the juvenile.

Harris hawks do not come cheap. Males cost approximately £300, with females up to £400.

The Goshawk (Accipiter gentilis)

The goshawk is the fastest and potentially the most talented of all hawks, but although the best-trained ones justify this reputation, not all have the ability to outfly a pheasant.

Goshawks are prone to fits, which can result in their death. Control and adjustment of their weight is imperative to their overall well-being, so no beginner or even intermediate falconer should contemplate using them. You would therefore be well advised to fly either a Harris hawk or a red-tail for two or more seasons before taking on this bird, which requires much more understanding.

Experienced falconers can have excellent hunting with a goshawk as their ability to fly a wide variety of game is potentially greater than that of other hawks.

A male goshawk will cost approximately £600 to £800, and a female up to a £1000.

The Sparrowhawk (Accipiter nisus)

Hunting with a sparrowhawk is for me the most exciting of all the experiences falconry has to offer. Their courage and enthusiasm combined with their ability make these little birds a favourite among today's experienced falconers.

They are similar in many ways to goshawks. Both are prone to throwing fits which can be life-threatening, and both have high metabolic rates. So if you wish to train one, you should have no doubt about the many difficulties that could arise. You will be entering into a new sphere of falconry and taking on a job that is as hard as any. Sparrowhawks are fragile and susceptible to the slightest weight-control mistakes. They should be weighed twice daily and handled frequently. Feeding should always be done on the fist, as throwing food to them could lead them eventually to carry quarry.

Only the falconer who has had a few seasons with a Harris hawk or the like and another season or two with a goshawk is in a position to work with a sparrowhawk. The female is a far better proposition than the male or musket, as it is physically more robust.

Sparrowhawks will cost approximately £100 for a musket and approximately £200 for a female.

The Kestrel (Falco tinnunculus)

The kestrel is not really suitable for falconry. It is extremely small, fragile and easily upset. They are rarely used as part of a display team, as very few show the interest or ability to perform to a high standard.

Kestrels are often sought after by beginners, as their low price makes them affordable for almost anyone. It is sad that this should be the case, because if you fly this species just for a little fun, you risk killing or losing your bird if you fail to establish the right flying weight. If she is too high you will lose her, and if she is too low she will easily die. Flying a bird of this kind allows you no margin of error. Kestrels should therefore be left to falconers who have gained considerable expertise in measuring weight control.

The main diet of a wild kestrel consists of worms, mice, voles and insects, none of which is palatable to humans. Some beginners believe they can train their bird to catch rabbits, but this is just not possible.

Kestrels will cost approximately £100 for either male or female.

The European Eagle-owl (Bubo bubo)

Generally, owls do not make good hunting birds. They are very rarely seen on field meets, as their limited ability discourages falconers from owning them. They do not possess the speed and majesty associated with hawks, and they are often undecided about chasing quarry. Their stamina is often questionable, and they have endless annoying habits whilst in the field.

However, if you have a love of owls, the European eagle-owl may offer an interesting proposition. Being the largest of all the owls, the larger female has the ability to fly foxes, and some falconers use them solely for this purpose. They have a sound temperament, and, considering their massive size, they are quite gentle. But because of their limited field achievements, you should be aware that serious falconry may not be possible.

European eagle-owls will cost approximately £200 for a male and about £250 for a female.

A Harris hawk
A goshawk

A sparrowhawk
A kestrel

ABOVE: *A Bengal eagle-owl*

RIGHT: *A barn owl*

ABOVE: *A European eagle-owl*

The Bengal Eagle-owl (Bengal bengalensis)

For those who want to fly an owl but think the European eagle-owl is slightly too large, the Bengal may be a better proposition. Although it is quite a lot smaller, it is still a powerful bird that may give you limited sport.

Bengals can have an extremely inconsistent temperament even when fully hand-reared. Like most owls, they lack enthusiasm, and are often happy to achieve nothing. This is not to say that they are totally useless; it simply means you may have to try a number of birds until you acquire one that shows any potential. Very few falconers fly them.

Bengal eagle-owls cost approximately £120 to £150 for either a male or a female.

The Barn Owl (Tyto alba)
Barn owls are often looked upon as good pets for children, which is a misconception, as their cuteness and potential tameness is overshadowed by their need for frequent exercise.

Over the years I have had many barn owls, some good and some not so good. The ones that have shown reasonable ability have been used as part of my display team and as an aid in educating the public about the commitment needed to keep such a bird, whilst the others have been maintained and exercised privately to a suitable standard.

As I have said, no bird of prey or owl is suitable purely as a pet. Unless you have very good reason to possess a barn owl, then do not buy one. Pet shop owners will gladly sell you one – even one that has not been hand-reared – but it will only be a liability as you will never tame it. Moreover, the diet of a wild barn owl consists mainly of small rodents, insects etc., and larger quarry is completely out of their grasp.

In summary, owls are a poor proposition compared to hawks, although they are used for flying displays as they are a firm favourite amongst the public.

Barn owls will cost upwards of £30 for either male or female.

Imprints

An imprint is a bird that has been reared by means other than its biological or foster parents.

The three common types of imprint are the food imprint, the social imprint, and the crèche-reared imprint.

The Food Imprint
Any bird which is described as a food imprint should be avoided at all costs. She will have been reared in complete isolation, which means that whenever you are in sight, she will scream for your attention and demand to be fed. She is also likely to scream when she can hear the sound of human voices, associating them with food and play. She may be sticky-footed which is an annoying habit. This occurs when one requires to cast the bird from the fist and she attempts to cling onto the glove with her talons, and during training her comprehension and lack of fear for humans could make her turn nasty if she is upset. She is likely to mantle over food by spreading her wings and scream if she feels threatened by anyone or anything that may try to take her meal away. Carrying quarry, which is one of the

falconer's worst nightmares, is a problem all too often associated with this imprint.

The Social Imprint

A social imprint is a bird that has been reared by hand in isolation. Unlike the food imprint, she will spend much of her time in the company of the breeder, and depend on him for food and socialising. She will not generally scream as the falconer attends to her every need.

Social imprints will not breed with their own kind but they are ideally suited to artificial insemination in later life. During training and hunting you may experience similar difficulties to those encountered with the food imprint, but probably to a lesser degree.

The Crèche-reared Imprint

This is the most common variety of imprint. The crèche-reared imprint is the outcome of a group of babies that have been hatched via an incubator and hand-reared from the egg. The young never see their parents or foster parents but spend all their time in each other's company. They will breed with their own kind and, unlike the social or food imprint, will grow up believing they are hawks and not humans. Generally, the crèche-reared imprint will not realise that the falconer is hand-feeding them as, in their very early days, he will wear a glove. As a result, the young will not see the falconer as being a food provider which should eliminate the possibility of their screaming for food. However, if the rearing is not carried out correctly, such birds may turn out to be aggressive and to scream and mantle over food in much the same way as the food imprint.

Although many falconers fly imprints, I do not recommend that you start your falconry career with one, as you cannot be sure how a bird reared in this way may turn out. You may find she is inconsistent during training, leading to poor ability whilst attempting to fly quarry. The red-tailed buzzard, in particular, will be extremely dangerous to handle and untrustworthy.

Generally speaking, longwings, shortwings and broadwings are kept with their parents until they are at least 12 weeks old. They are then known as being totally or fully parent-reared. This means they are unlikely to develop the bad habits often associated with imprints. Because falconers have been buying parent-reared birds for many years, we have not only developed a good understanding of their training and hunting potential, but more importantly, we have a far greater understanding of their likely behaviour pattern.

Owls, on the other hand, are different. You should purchase a baby at two weeks old and take over the tedious job of the parents. This entails hand-feeding, socialising and welcoming the bird into your home as part of the family. If you buy a young owl which is fully parent-reared, you will have a bird that is aggressive, easily upset and one that can never be trusted.

I have bought lanners, luggers and saker falcons at six weeks old, which allowed me to partly imprint them, and I find that this is fine for flying displays and pest control. But for the pursuit of falconry, I will always purchase a parent-reared eyass.

Many beginners believe that a bird which has been hand-reared will be easier to train, friendlier and almost impossible to lose. In fact, imprints are extremely temperamental and even the most experienced falconer would not welcome the unpredictability of training and working them. I have seen the owners of such birds being footed and bitten, and I once saw an imprinted Harris hawk fly directly from a tree and hit the falconer behind the head whilst he was beating bushes for quarry. These sorts of incidents are extremely dangerous, and to me it is not the way to conduct falconry. One must be able to trust one's hawk totally, but never forget the power, speed and agility that a fit hunting bird possesses and the damage that can be done.

You would be well advised therefore to find a reputable breeder and ask specifically for a fully parent-reared eyass. She will be easier to train, she should not scream for either food or attention and she will perform far more consistently in the field.

Hybrids

A hybrid bird is the result of crossbreeding two different species, usually longwings. The semen is taken from the tiercel, the male peregrine, and artificially inseminated into a female of one's choice. Although some would say this is a major breakthrough in captive breeding, I have reservations. In my opinion, it involves creating a 'superbird', a bird with more ability and agility than is natural, which could tilt the odds greatly in favour of the bird making more kills. This is not to say that hybrids are supersonic hunting machines, of course; I believe the breeders are simply trying to give the bird and falconer optimum ammunition to take into the field. Although I have never flown such a falcon, I have friends who have and, it has to be said, most fly and perform extremely well.

Crossbreeding does not affect the birds' health, nor does it make them unpredictable. They pose no major danger to their handler and seem to train up pretty much like any parent-reared eyass.

CHAPTER FIVE

Looking After Your Bird

In my opinion, falconry cannot be compared with any other field sport. Novices have to learn an awful lot if they are to succeed. To be successful you must always put the well-being of your bird first; her needs should come before your own. Although this book may be useful in giving you advice about what to do and when, you will not truly appreciate the depth of commitment involved until you acquire your first bird. You will be judged by others by your approach to the sport and to your bird.

As I have said, there are many people who would love to see falconry banned, along with other field sports. We cannot begin to defend the sport if we do not look after our birds and the countryside we walk and fly over, to the best of our ability. Those who do only give the sport a bad name, and its opponents valuable ammunition.

I believe that the way forward for falconry is for falconers to work together. Although we will all have different opinions on various aspects of the sport, which can only be a good thing, we should all find the time to advise and help newcomers. Even those who have only been a part of the sport for a season or two can do so much to help, guide, and advise those just starting.

Unfortunately, there is no compulsory apprenticeship scheme in Great Britain. Anyone can buy a bird of prey; it is as easy as buying a puppy. We can only hope that those who do so have the sense to realise that the care of a bird of prey is intensely demanding.

I would like to see falconry clubs and associations made more easily available to the public, as I believe they can be very influential. The British Falconers' Club is one which is accessible, and which is dedicated to helping beginners. It runs an apprenticeship scheme, under which you will be guided by people who have been practising falconers for many years. You will be able to attend regular field meets throughout the hawking season, where you will have the opportunity of furthering your basic knowledge. Being part of a well-established club, and having the chance of associating with falconers of sound knowledge and practical ability is the best preparation for the beginner.

The care of a bird of prey involves committing yourself to daily health and safety checks. You also owe it to your bird to see that she receives a bath every two days or so, and she will need exercising as often as possible. Her weathering will have to be scrubbed and hosed clean two or three times a week, whilst keeping her feather-perfect

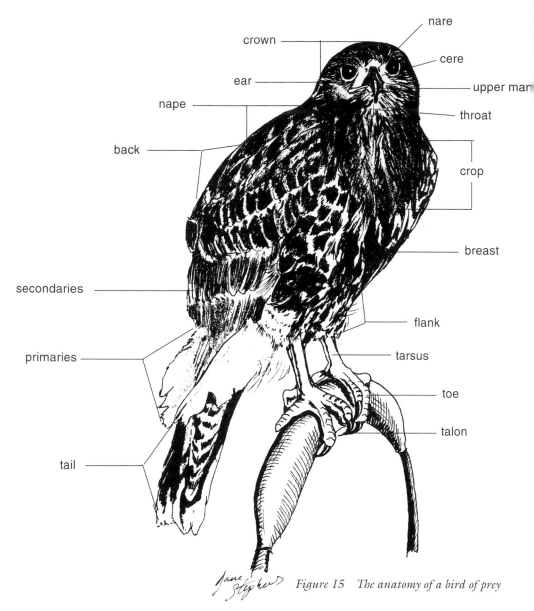

Figure 15   The anatomy of a bird of prey

will be a constant undertaking. This is not something to be undertaken merely through a casual interest.

Raptor Anatomy

If you have ever listened to a conversation between falconers you may have wondered whether they are talking another language. There are special terms to describe just about everything to do with keeping, training and hunting birds of prey, from those that relate to the birds themselves to those that describe aspects of their maintenance. But none are more important than the terms which describe the parts of a bird's anatomy. An understanding of that anatomy and the words used in connection with it, is essential and you have a duty to learn them all.

At the Eagle-Owl School of Falconry, we feel so strongly that beginners should understand the different terms, that we use the correct falconry terminology right from the start. We will explain the meanings thoroughly, but only once. Towards the end of the course there is a little written exam. Students do not know about it; it is sprung on them. But I am delighted to say that by the time of the exam most students are quite familiar with the majority of terms.

Figure 15 shows a Harris hawk with the most important parts of the body marked. Try to memorise them until you are fully proficient.

Weathering Checks

Assuming that you have built your weathering to a good, robust standard, it should remain maintenance-free for many years. However, it is worth getting into the habit of checking it thoroughly each day and examining it for defects.

At times of incessant high winds, make sure that the weathering has not moved or subsided slightly. High wind can destroy much hardier constructions than those made from larch-lap. The major concern will be the roof. There is a certain amount of movement in all wooden constructions, and the roof may stretch and split the felt. This will gradually let water into the weathering. So keep the necessary materials handy for emergency repairs. Also look out for bubbling and/or pimpling of the felt. This is a major worry as it could mean that water has found its way under the felt. If it is not immediately rectified the roofing boards will rot.

Although a roof probably will not leak as a result of prolonged rainfall, it could do so during heavy snow. The snow will lie on the roof, and could cause problems as it begins to thaw. Thick deposits will also put an extra burden on the roof, so any snow that settles should be removed.

The larch-lap panels can also be a problem, as they often tend to move during rain, snow and high winds. If you have not felted the panels externally, check regularly that this has not occurred, and if it has, make the necessary repairs. Also make sure that the paving slabs around the base of the weathering are not displaced or broken.

Even though the wire-fronted section of the weathering is of a good, thick gauge, it can still be damaged by inquisitive vermin and by repeated movement of the door or the structure itself. Even high winds can do some damage. Check daily that the wire is securely fixed to the frame, making sure that the welded sections have not come loose and weak.

The door is the obvious entry point for intruders, so all external screws should be checked for slackening, tightened regularly and, if necessary, replaced. Padlocks will need to be oiled occasionally, as there is often no warning when the inner parts cease to work. Always have a spare padlock available in case this happens.

Inspect the inside of the weathering to ensure that it is clean and free of foreign bodies or growths. I once had a snowy owl who fell victim to the fatal fungal disease, aspergilloses, which affects a hawk's lungs. The autopsy suggested that the cause was a fungus which was growing somewhere around the bird's living quarters. I checked the inside of the weathering thoroughly, and found a fine green moss spreading under a length of ageing timber which I had put there to make it look good.

You should thoroughly clean your weathering at least twice a week. The pea shingle and all mute-infected areas should be sprayed with Virkon S, a solution that kills bacteria. Allow it to penetrate before hosing it away. It is outstandingly effective, and is available from most equipment suppliers.

The weathering is your bird's home. You have a duty to keep it clean and safe. There is nothing worse than a weathering which contains hundreds of castings, dried mutes splashed on the wooden panels, pieces of rotten meat scattered on the pea shingle or a bath filled with filthy water. To keep a bird in this condition is extremely oppressive, and you run the risk of making her ill. Raptors and owls are naturally clean animals, so you have an obligation to maintain and clean their quarters on a regular basis.

A wooden construction will not last for ever, no matter how well it is maintained. Sooner or later it will have to be demolished and replaced by a newer, sturdier construction. Just like a garden shed, it will eventually rot and become a potential danger to the bird inside. Similarly with felt – it does not come with a lifetime guarantee. The roof will need to be thoroughly checked long before the beginning of each winter.

Equipment Checks

The maintenance of your falconry equipment should be just as important as the care of your bird. Falconry furniture and accessories can be very expensive; to make them last, they will have to be looked after and kept thoroughly clean.

Never leave perches outdoors, especially overnight. You should lacquer blocks annually to protect them from rain and prevent damp from penetrating into and rotting the wood, and the leather perching part of some bows should be regularly oiled as this will nurture and revive the pores. Bow perches that are finished in cord binding may be ruined by urban pests if they are left outside, as will items such as creances, lures and leashes. Leather lure pads will also need oiling from time to time, again to nurture the pores, which soon become brittle.

When you pick your bird up for the first time each morning, you should ensure that her equipment is in a good state and still fit to be used. You should immediately renew anything that is worn or damaged and thoroughly clean anything that is soiled.

First check the anklets and jesses. If there are no signs that your bird has been picking at the leather overnight, and if both are free from dried faeces and still supple, go on to check the swivel. This should show no signs of wear; once again it must be free from dried faeces and mud. It must not be distorted in any way as a result of overnight bating. Check that it is still spinning freely and smoothly and make sure that the jesses have not slipped so that they prevent the lower eye from turning. This can have devastating effects.

The leash should have no *Equipment checks*

weaknesses from overnight picking. Run your hand along the full length of the cord, looking and feeling for problems. The condition of the top knot in particular will tell you whether a leash has reached the end of its constructive life. Check the perch for any deterioration, making sure the tethering ring has not worn and the perching point is clean and undamaged. Items such as hardened anklets, damaged perch surfaces or worn lures could cause abrasions to your bird's tarsus or feet, which will make perching uncomfortable. Defective jesses, swivel, leash and creance could lead to your losing your bird. And you could cause yourself unnecessary discomfort, if not nasty cuts, from poorly maintained items such as the gauntlet.

Every item you will need during the day should also be checked. If you are training your bird, make sure that there are no signs of weakness in your creance, as this could enable your bird to break free.

If you travel with your hawk in a wooden box, check that the internal perch is robust, clean and in good order. Both types of lure must be examined for sharp, damaging sections which could harm a bird's feet on impact. Examine your glove for damage to the stitching and make sure that the hanging tassel or brass D-ring is in good order, especially if it is regularly used for tying the bird to. If you use a hood, make sure it is in faultless condition. Finally, check the bag to ensure that the meat pouch is clean and the stitching is in good order. The strap or belt should show no sign of wear as you would have problems if the buckle broke whilst you were in the field.

Before you set off for a day's training or hunting, be sure that you have with you all the items you could possibly need. In the past, I have had a tendency to leave my whistle behind. Since I cannot whistle naturally, this has meant going back for it or wasting the day. Now I have a spare whistle hanging from the interior mirror of my vehicle at all times. Whistles are a vital item of equipment, and should be checked regularly for tone and clarity.

Good falconers take just as much pride in the appearance of their equipment as they do in their bird. Maintained furniture and accessories last a long time, and also say something about the way you conduct yourself. I cannot understand why some falconers carry a bag, for instance, that is long past its best both in appearance and practicality. Clean equipment gives a good impression of one's standards of professionalism. Falconry equipment does not last for ever; when the time comes, change unsightly and poor-quality items.

Bird Weighing

For a beginner, there is no daily duty more important than weighing your bird and accounting for any loss of weight. A great deal depends on your competence in this most vital area of hawk ownership, and the importance of checking the weight daily cannot be overemphasised. As we saw in the last chapter, it is imperative that you use only top-quality scales. They should be checked for accuracy every day and, if they use batteries, these should be changed regularly.

Maintaining your bird's flying weight is by far the hardest part of falconry. Her vitality and continued good health are entirely in your hands, so it is essential that you develop the skill and knowledge to do it properly.

During the flying season you should weigh your bird at the same time every day. This way you can be confident that she has an empty stomach. You should also be confident that she has cast a pellet; otherwise you will receive an erroneous reading, and may lose her when she is flown, as her desire to feed will be restricted. Always pick up her daily casting to verify that she has done so.

Before placing her on the scales, remove the leash and swivel, and ensure that, apart from her feet, no part of her torso is touching the scales, as this could also result in a false reading. Record the weight clearly in a log book and keep it safe for future reference.

There is a very fine line between a bird being overweight, underweight and at the correct flying weight. If she is overweight, you could easily lose her, whilst if she is underweight, you will reduce her ability to fly strongly and she may collapse. It is impossible to give an estimate of the weight a bird will need to lose before a flying weight is attained. The only way to arrive at the correct weight is by slow, controlled, accountable weight loss, and also by daily assessing her overall condition. Never take chances, and constantly look for the tell-tale signs that something is wrong.

If you have bought an eyass of the year, you should feel her breastbone as soon as you purchase her and get a mental picture of how it feels. This will help you to determine the amount of body fat at any one time. Although you will initially lack the experience to appreciate the precise difference between a sharp and a fat bone, you will soon be able to differentiate between the two by feeling it daily as you begin reducing the bird's weight.

You must also record the amount of food you give your bird each day. This way a pattern will soon emerge of how much holds her weight and how much makes her gain or lose weight. After a time the scales will act only as a back-up, confirming the physical assessment you have already made.

If you are unsure about your bird's state of health, you should immediately seek professional advice. Delay may have disastrous consequences. Your bird has a right to prompt medical attention, and it is your duty to see she receives it. There may be times when an

Weighing a hawk

unwell bird will need nursing around the clock. A very ill barn owl of mine once needed my undivided attention for a solid week. Fortunately I was in a position to give it to her. If I had had a nine-to-five job she would probably not have survived. Dilemmas like this must be fully considered before you buy a hawk, as afterwards, it may be too late.

Health Checks

It is vitally important that you check your bird daily for signs of sickness. Birds of prey are not immune to sudden, life-threatening illnesses, and you should register yourself and your hawk with a veterinary surgeon who has the knowledge and experience to tend to raptors.

Study your hawk each morning, initially observing her from outside the weathering. It is important that she is sitting astute upon the perch with her eyes wide open, bright and alert. If she is standing on one leg, it does not necessarily mean she is unwell; it may just be a sign that she is contented.

If she looks observant, go into the weathering and step her onto the fist for a closer examination. You should now check for a variety of things. Her nares should be clear, with no evident signs of discharge, there should be no foul smell coming from her mouth, and her cere

Checking the breastbone

must be unimpaired, as this could ultimately affect her breathing. Her feet should be clean, with no signs of redness or distension, which may indicate bumblefoot. Her tarsus should be free from abrasions or swelling, and you must check carefully beneath the anklets. Her upper and lower mandible should not be cracked or chipped, which can sometimes be caused either by the hard bones of her diet or by the intake of pea shingle particles.

The casting must be clear, with no traces of blood, and her mutes should be black and white, with no signs of diarrhoea. Mutes tell us a great deal about how a bird is feeling. If they are green, it could suggest that no food has passed through her stomach since she last ate. Yellow mutes are fine if a sick bird is on antibiotics, but brown ones may be an indication of too rich a diet. Mutes containing traces of blood could indicate a worm infection or else a bird that is stressed or traumatised.

Her plumage should feel clean to the touch, with an overall appearance of shininess. Whilst she is sitting on your gloved hand, begin moving your arm up and down. She will naturally open her wings, and you can check that they are working correctly and that there are no abrasions on the under-parts. It is also important to check for crooked or broken feathers, as they may need imping or straightening. Any hardened faeces or dirt on the feathers should be delicately cleaned off with lukewarm water and a touch of baby oil before she is flown.

There are important signs that will tell you immediately if your bird is unwell or critically underweight. Her eyes will be screwed up, without their accustomed alertness, her breastbone may feel extremely sharp, she will be reluctant to do her daily tasks, her bating will be weak and tiresome and she may be standing lazily on one leg with her head resting on her wings.

A loss of appetite is very unusual for a bird of prey at flying weight, and this is a major sign of possible illness. Sudden loss of weight is also uncharacteristic in a healthy bird. Weight loss can tell us a great deal about a bird's health. Inexplicable loss of weight is a sure sign of something wrong, possibly a worm infestation. Even if you are reducing fat weight to establish a flying weight, there should never be any rapid, unaccountable loss of weight.

If it is obvious that your bird is in poor condition, handle her as little as possible, and then with extreme care. Prepare a cardboard box containing a cushion or blanket as a soft lining. Establish the bird's current weight by laying her on the scales if she is too weak to stand. Make sure you write the recording down as you do not want to repeat the process. Then place her carefully in the box, and put it under a heat lamp or near a radiator. The room should be made as dark and quiet as possible. Try not to handle the bird any more, as you will only stress her unnecessarily. Avoid anything that is likely to upset her. Once you have settled her, assess the situation as best you can before telephoning the vet for advice.

Approximately four times a year, you should worm your bird with something like Panacure. This is particularly important both before she goes down for the moult and directly afterwards. She should also be sprayed before and after the moult with a pyrethrum-based insecticide. Johnsons' Anti-Mite is ideal, and is available from veterinary surgeries and good pet shops.

After a short time, you will develop an understanding of your bird and be able to recognise any causes for worry. The more time you spend with her the better you will get to know her and appreciate her different moods, which is essential if you are to assess her state of fitness before she is flown free. If you are ever in doubt about her health, do not fly her.

Diet

This section describes the most common varieties of food fed to birds of prey and owls today. Their cost is to a certain extent dependent on whether it is delivered directly to your freezer or whether you collect it.

Chicks
Cockerels culled at a day old and sold either fresh or blast-frozen are the most common food source for hawks. They are readily available and extremely reasonably priced. But although most birds will readily eat chicks, they lack vital vitamins, which means that they should not be used as the sole diet. These vitamins can, however, be given in the form of SA 37 or Ace High supplements.

Chicks that have not been properly frozen run the risk of salmonella contamination. This is deadly to all birds of prey even if it is promptly diagnosed. You should therefore always buy this source of food from a reputable outlet. You can expect to pay approximately £3–4 per hundred. I would suggest however that you buy them in boxes of 250 or 300. This may work out a little cheaper.

Quail
These small birds are a first-class food source for birds of prey. Many breeders use quails exclusively when rearing a clutch of young. Their good protein and roughage content helps the bird to cast a pellet and is far superior to that of the fur and protein found in day-old cockerels.

Many falconers now breed their own quail, as they are very expensive to buy – they will cost approximately 50p each.

Pigeons
These birds are classed as vermin and are not easy to get hold of. They are available from shooting people, who are normally glad for you to take them away, but do make sure that you remove *all* lead shot before feeding them to your bird (see page 129). The heads and guts must also be carefully removed.

Pigeons carry trichomoniasis, a nasty disease which affects the mouths of birds of prey. You should therefore never feed it fresh; it requires a lengthy period in the freezer first. Few falconers feed pigeon and fewer feed feral pigeon. It is not a vital food source so not to feed it at all is no injustice.

Hares
Birds of prey often lose out with hare, as it normally ends up on the falconer's own table! It is nutritious, however, and will be good for your bird. The meat is dark and rich, so you should be careful about feeding your bird large amounts as it could take her over flying weight.

Hares are normally caught during the season by the bird itself. If it is your first season and you want to feed your bird hare, you may find that a colleague will spare you a little.

Rabbits

Rabbit flesh is very pale compared with hare, and is therefore less nutritious. Like chick, it is another main food source for many birds, as abundant quantities are caught throughout the hawking season and frozen to provide food all year round. More rabbit meat will have to be fed to hold your bird at flying weight compared with quails and rodents, and a hawk that is worked hard throughout the season will need a much better food source than rabbit, which does not have a great deal of nutritional value.

Rabbits are hard to come by unless you are able to acquire them by means of hawking or shooting. And if you use shot rabbits, do ensure that all lead shot is removed (see page 129). Some food outlets stock them at a cost of approximately £2–3 each.

Rodents

Rats and mice are an excellent food source for birds of prey and owls, and are easy to obtain from good food outlets. They are both high in protein and adequate in aiding a bird with her casting. Birds will do very well fed exclusively on them, and there will be no need for any artificial supplements. Most falconers discard the internal organs of rats, however, as hawks do not find them palatable.

Rodents are not normally bought singly but in packs. Rats come in packs of 25, at a price of about £25. In my opinion, mice are the best food source on the market, and birds that are fed on them for a long time tend to look and do extremely well. But they are expensive. They are normally sold in packs of 100, at a price of approximately £40. It is important to buy your rodents from a specialised outlet as those bought in a pet shop are expensive – sometimes more than double the price. Many falconers are now breeding their own mice which, if done on a large scale, can save a lot of money.

Liver

Liver is a good food for a sick hawk. It is easily obtained and contains many beneficial minerals, especially iron. Cut into small pieces, it is easy for a bird to swallow and digest. It should not be fed as part of a normal diet, however, but reserved for weak birds.

Beef

Beef is ideal when training a bird of prey. Feeding beef from the fist will not cause an outcry if members of the public see you doing it, as feeding a chick, mouse or rat could well do. It is easily obtained and is a clean food source for hawks. Although it lacks calcium and roughage, this can easily be provided in supplements. Shin is the most practical cut, as it is inexpensive and not too brittle. All fat should be carefully removed.

Before feeding beef to a young bird, you should slash a healthy piece into good-sized sections, so that when the bird eventually bends her head to accept a mouthful via the fist, she is encouraged by the size and ease of pull.

Squirrels:
Very few falconers feed their hawks this meat as it is tough and extremely difficult for a bird to break into. The practical way to acquire squirrel is for your bird to catch it herself.

Although squirrel hawking can produce excellent flights, falconers have reservations about it as a squirrel can give a hawk quite a nasty bite. The meat is not highly nutritious, so it does not matter if you do not feed it at all.

Gamebirds
Like hare, gamebirds tend to end up on the falconer's own table. Although they are nutritious they are far too delicious to allow a bird a look in. However, a good bird that has performed well throughout the season should be rewarded with more than just an occasional head.

Feeding a Healthy Mixed Diet
One very important skill that every novice must master is correct feeding. It is vital that your bird receives the right amount and kind of food, not only to sustain the correct flying weight but to keep her healthy, strong and flying fit. Understanding the nutritional values of her food is therefore essential.

I believe that birds of prey are no different from ourselves. Like us, they would only appreciate monotonous food if they are not aware that there is a variety available. Falconers have a vast selection of foods to choose from; some are packed with goodness whilst others are cheap that lack certain ingredients. You should see to it that your bird receives mixed foods of a high standard throughout her working or breeding career.

During initial training, beef is ideal, and is used by many falconers; the only drawback is the low level of calcium and roughage. Roughage is easily supplied by pulling the fur off a rat or the feathers from a quail and adding them to the beef. To add calcium you could use a supplement, or better still combine a rat's head with the beef.

Without doubt the most popular food used by falconers today are dead day-old cockerels. Some people feed their birds solely on these, adding a vitamin supplement, as explained on page 107. If you maintain a healthy mixed diet, however, following a consistent feeding pattern, there should never be any need to use supplements, as the food you use should contain all the goodness your bird requires. You should therefore only need supplements in special circumstances. Not only will an eyass of the year which is fed solely on chick be at a disadvantage as regards the quality of her food, but you could find it very difficult to get her to accept a change, which could cause problems if you were to run out of chicks.

Day-old chicks are no more than a dreary junk food, and to use them as the only food source is not fair to your bird. Whilst she is attempting to fly quarry, she will need quality food inside her, and she will not get this from chicks, as she would from mice, rats or quail. Chicks contain minimal protein and very little energy; they also contain a yolk sac saturated in cholesterol, which will eventually discolour a bird's feet and cere, so the sac should always be removed before feeding the chick to your bird. Personally, I am so opposed to chicks that I very rarely feed them to my birds. The ones in our freezers are primarily reserved for our working ferrets. In my opinion, a hawk fed exclusively on them is no different from a top athlete who eats only sweets or hamburgers; performance will inevitably suffer. In the case of a young bird, body fat will not quickly change into muscle, her bones will always be a bit brittle, especially if reared this way, and she will always struggle to find her much-needed stamina.

Beginners have often told me that their birds will not accept anything other than chick, but this is because they have been fed them for so long that they find them too palatable to change to anything heavier, like rodents. If a bird will not accept a change to a better diet, then she should go without. Her hunger will always get the better of her in the end.

Hopefully, your newly acquired eyass will have been reared on rodents or quail, as this is a good basis from which to begin her arduous and lengthy working career. Top breeders often boast that their young are brought up solely on this kind of food, as it is a very good selling point, and you should look out for this claim when choosing a breeder.

The chart below is a typical weekly diet for Athene, a two-year-old female hunting Harris hawk.

Sun.	Caught rabbit; allowed her to feed up.
Mon.	Rest day. Too heavy to fly. No food.
Tue.	Mice.
Wed.	Quail.
Thur.	Rat.
Fri.	Mice.
Sat.	Quail.
Sun.	Caught hare; allowed her to feed up.

Because her daily intake is highly nutritious, I have to be extremely careful that she does not become overweight. Therefore, she will not need the quantity of food she would require from alternative foods such as rabbit or chick.

A bird of prey is only as good as the fuel inside her. Feeding adequate quantities of food with mixed nutritional values is vital in helping her to achieve success in a very challenging field.

Food Preparation
The preparation of your bird's food is a very important part of caring for her. Cleanliness is vital to maintaining a healthy bird. Some falconers do not appreciate the significance of basic food hygiene, but it is essential that you prepare and present meals to your bird cleanly.

Pieces of meat and dirty utensils such as knives, chopping boards and trays will attract flies, so they should not be left lying around. Utensils that come into contact with food ought to be sterilised and thoroughly washed immediately after each use. You should also wash your hands before preparing food, and clean and cover any cuts or abrasions. If necessary, wear gloves, especially if you suffer from dermatitis or similar skin disorders. Do not smoke during preparation; those who do so are not carrying out their duties acceptably.

Knives should be sharpened regularly to make cutting and gutting easier.

This level may seem a little excessive, especially when raptors in the wild do not enjoy this standard of hygiene. However we are in a position to give our birds the best, and as a result they usually live longer, happier and healthier lives than their wild cousins.

I would not recommend you to feed carrion or road-side casualties to your bird. They may have died from an infectious disease which could be transmitted to your bird. Even animals killed by traffic are often ill, which is why they are hit. There is always a risk when you feed your bird such food, and I believe it is not one worth taking. Resist the temptation to feed food where the history is questionable. So only if you have shot or hunted the animal yourself, or it has been killed by your bird can you be fairly confident that it is clean and free from disease. However, quarry that has been shot with a twelve-bore should never be given to a bird; lead shot is poisonous and could easily harm a bird's gut (see page 129). If it has been killed with a 22 air rifle it should not present any problems, provided the shot is located and removed first.

Remember that some foods such as rats and pigeons should be gutted before being fed to your bird, as the internal organs could be carrying a disease. Then either seal them in a heavy-duty, scented, plastic bag or burn them immediately to avoid a maggot infestation.

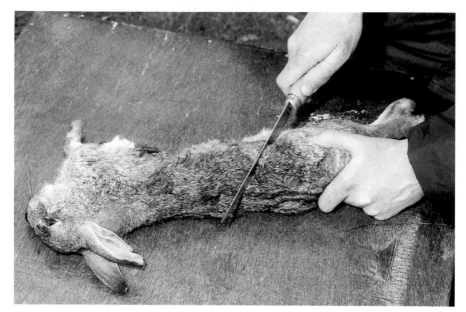

Preparing rabbit

This also applies to any food which the bird has left from the previous day.

I believe that careful food preparation is one of the most important aspects of hawk ownership. Too many falconers neglect it, but I am confident that birds sustained on a healthy, mixed, clean diet will do far better than those which are not.

Imping

The word used by falconers to describe feather management is imping. It is a traditional art which requires dexterity, and is one that you must master, as your bird is unlikely to go through a complete season without snapping at least one vital flight feather. It is an aspect of bird care that is often overlooked by novices and intermediate falconers, which is a pity, for a bird's feathers are one of a multitude of important elements which give her the ability to perform.

There are a number of ways in which a vital feather can become damaged. It can happen whilst your bird is being manned and going through the stage of thrashing about erratically whenever you are in sight, but more often than not, it occurs as a result of flying quarry. Whatever the cause, whenever damage is apparent, you must cease flying and undertake repairs immediately.

A damaged feather shows up in different ways. It could be suspended from the tip or midway down the shaft, it could be severely bent or it could be completely broken. Moreover, a bird which is not accustomed to a tail-mount will often pick and tug at it until finally a deck feather is completely pulled out. Different injuries require different approaches. Modern materials are available to make the job easier, but I strongly recommend that before attempting to replace or repair a feather you receive expert, practical tuition, which probably means attending a course.

Imping is a complex subject, but I shall explain some of the basic guidelines which must be followed. The falconer is mainly concerned with well-balanced flight feathers which are in good condition – the primaries, the secondaries and the tail feathers are the all-important ones. These feathers give the bird optimum balance, manoeuvrability and control. If your bird were to injure a primary, and it had to be replaced, you would need to find a corresponding feather, either from the same species or from a similar one, which was more or less the same size and from the same side of the torso. You could therefore not use a feather from a female on a male as there would be

Coping overgrown talons

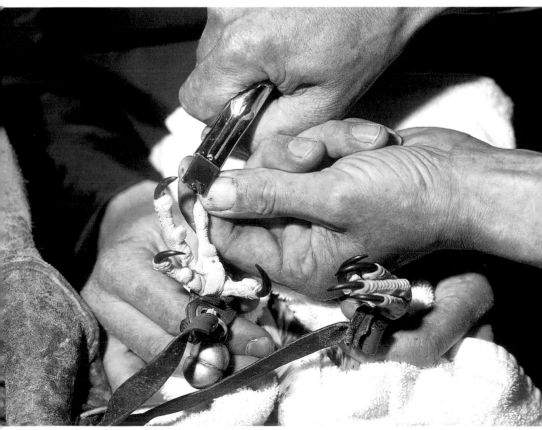

a significant difference in size and shape. Ideally, you should aim to use a feather that has been dropped by the same bird in a previous moult, as the match would be more or less perfect. Unfortunately, you cannot do this with tail feathers as they grow notably longer after a bird's initial moult.

I have from time to time seen birds with all sorts of feathers missing, while some have been hanging by a mere thread and others have been matted in dried mud. Not only does this make a bird look untidy, but it restricts her ability to fly. A raptor can be in tip-top condition, healthy and flying fit, but if her plumage is not right she will always struggle, and this may make all the difference to her making a kill.

The hardiness of a bird's feathers will differ significantly from one species to another, depending on its country of origin. Most birds, however, have quite brittle feathers in their first year, and imping becomes more necessary. Although feathers become naturally harder as a bird reaches adulthood, you should assess your bird's plumage daily.

Coping

Coping is the art of attending to a bird of prey's beak and talons. It requires various skills, as you must have a good eye for shape and design, a professional touch and a steady hand. It is probably among the hardest of all skills to develop, often taking many seasons to master. Under no circumstances should you try to do it yourself until you have the requisite skill, as you run the risk of making the defects worse and possibly causing unnecessary pain. If you attend a falconry course you will be taken through the correct procedures, and you must be confident that you understand them fully.

In the wild, birds of prey keep their beaks and talons in order naturally, as a result of the food they eat and the surfaces they perch on. Although they will also do so to a certain extent in captivity, it is not quite the same.

For a beginner, the hardest part of coping is probably knowing when to do it, as it is not easy to decide when the beak and talons are the correct length and when they are overgrown. My advice is to take a close-up photograph as soon as you buy your bird; this way you will always have a point of reference. As a general rule, however, the beak should not need attention until just before the first moult. There are obviously exceptions to this. If a bird were to crack her beak, you would need to attend to it immediately, in order to prevent further deterioration.

You may find that a damaged beak will need filing several times to iron out the defect; even the slightest perforation will often require ongoing attention. I once had a kestrel which cracked her upper mandible severely on one side. I had no alternative but to disfigure the bird by cutting a large section of the damaged beak away. This enabled me to get to the root of the problem and after continual filing and shaping, her beak grew back healthy and strong. If I had left the defect, she would probably have lost her beak, leading to all sorts of complications. It is important that a bird has a beak which feels comfortable and balanced, as otherwise it may affect her ability to pull and eat certain foods.

Compared with the beak, attending to the talons is not too difficult. The most important thing to remember is to prevent you from injuring yourself. It is, therefore, wise to have an assistant who is capable of casting a bird correctly. Ideally, talons should have their tips snipped back, preferably before the bird is taken home from the breeder, as this will greatly reduce the risk of her piercing her own feet, which could in turn, lead to bumblefoot (see pages 126-7).

It is important to have all the correct equipment for coping. This is:

1. a suitable set of needle files for shaping
2. clippers for cutting – I recommend the type used by vets, which are made from stainless steel and will retain their cutting edge for a considerable period
3. a silver nitrate stick, available from chemists and veterinary surgeries, which will ease the flow of blood and soothe the injury if you clip a talon or beak too short.

When you are coping the beak, the bird must be carefully laid, breast down, on a cushion, as this will give her something soft to grip. When cutting talons, I prefer to lay the bird on her back, extending the legs upright. It is vital that coping of both the beak and the talons is done quickly and efficiently, so as to minimise stress.

Coping is a skill that every owner must develop. All too often I have seen upper mandibles cracked and caked in dry decaying food matter. This normally occurs when the owner does not deal with the overgrowth soon enough or does not have the knowledge or ability to perform the task. You cannot expect to be able to do it fresh from a falconry course, so you should join a club and get help from other members.

The Annual Moult

Raptors and owls moult every year, and it is vital to the growth of new feathers that the moult goes smoothly. Under no circumstances should you fly your bird, deprive her of food or subject her to unnecessary stress during this period, as this could result in the new feathers being deformed, brittle and unsightly. You will have a significant influence over the moulting process, so you must be aware of what contributes to a successful moult.

There are two principal factors that set the moult going: the changing day-length and the amount of food eaten. As the short, cold, days of winter give way to longer, warmer spring-time ones, a bird of prey's internal timepiece will tell her to begin dropping feathers. This is around late March to early April. You must give her extra food in order to get the process going. If, during this period, a bird is held at a strict flying weight, the moult will not commence. As you need your bird to drop old feathers and grow new ones in time for the following hawking season, there is no logical point in delaying. During March, therefore, you should stop flying and begin to take your bird's weight steadily up.

During the moult, feathers are dropped in sequence, generally in matched pairs and at certain intervals. The falconer is particularly concerned with the growth of strong flight feathers, such as primaries and secondaries as well as the tail feathers, as these give the bird optimum manoeuvrability and the ability to fly powerfully. You should gather all the old feathers, if they are in good condition, and keep them safely stored, as you may need to use them for imping during the following hunting season.

The approximate time from the dropping of a feather until the new one has grown down and hardened off is approximately seven weeks, and from beginning to end the moulting process takes around five or six months. This is rather a bleak time for falconers, as it seems to drag on and on. Where weekends had once been taken up attending field meets, one now has a major gap in the calendar, which somehow needs to be filled. The last hawking day of the season is always a sad time, for we are all aware that the next meet will not be for many months. However, there are a few advantages to a bird being inactive throughout the summer. During this period, trees are in full leaf, so it becomes difficult to spot one's bird, ground cover is extensive, making it hard to see quarry such as rabbit, the game will be out of season (see page 151), and the hot days will make hunting stressful for the bird.

Although it is possible for a bird to moult satisfactorily whilst tethered to her perch, it is preferable to allow her the freedom of the weathering. This way, she will get a little exercise, thus preventing boredom. You should place a variety of perching points in the weathering, making sure not to overcrowd it. Position them at various heights and locations so that the bird can hop freely from one to another. Keep them away from door openings, food shoots and any allocated bath space, as you will be visiting these frequently. The swivel and leash should be removed, but personally I like to keep the jesses on in case I need to catch the bird quickly with minimal fuss. I do, however, switch from mews to flying jesses to avoid tangling.

If your bird is allowed the freedom of the weathering, mutes, castings and decaying food will be scattered over a wide area. This will attract flies, so it is vitally important to clean the weathering frequently to prevent maggot infestation.

The most important thing during any hot spell is to see that your bird has access to fresh water. If she is allowed the freedom of the weathering, however, she will often mute in her water before taking a drink. You should avoid going into her quarters unnecessarily, so you should cut a trap door in the weathering a little larger than the bath itself. You can then withdraw the bath for cleaning, without upsetting the bird.

During the growth of a new feather, the sheath or quill is filled with blood, and as the feather grows, so the blood is reduced. This is when the webbing becomes visible. At this stage feathers are extremely fragile and if they are sufficiently knocked they may bleed or snap. You should ensure that these new feathers do not develop deformities, such as fret marks or hunger traces.

Figure 16 shows examples of deformed feathers. The first is a pinched feather. This occurs when a raptor has been upset during the growth of a new feather. The second shows hunger traces, which will become apparent if the bird has not had enough food whilst her new feathers grow. The feather does not appear to be consistently smooth along the webbing. Fret marks, as shown in the third example, occur when a bird has been disturbed and upset during the growth of a new feather. It will consist of dark ugly bars running horizontally along the length of the webbing.

Before a bird is put down for the moult, she should be sprayed for mites and wormed, and if necessary her beak and talons should be coped. She should be given a clean bill of health and monitored every day until the moult is complete. You should also gather the dropped feathers, as this will help you determine when your bird has finished moulting.

A hawk that remains sufficiently tame and relaxed during this period can be offered a bath on the weathering lawn, provided it is quiet and she is unlikely to become stressed. An experienced falconer will know if this is practicable or not.

On completion of the moult, the bird must be weighed to establish the new fat weight, and once again she should be sprayed for mites and wormed. If necessary, her beak and talons should be coped, and new equipment – anklets, jesses, swivel and leash – should be ready for her. You can now begin to reduce the fat weight to attain a new flying and hunting weight. It is worth mentioning that a bird will fly

Figure 16   Deformed feathers

a little heavier in her second year than she did in her first, so you must not take it for granted that the first season's flying weight is acceptable.

Your bird will not have completely forgotten the lessons that you taught her in her immature year, so you will find that the amount of manning and training required is significantly reduced, and she will be ready for the field in a fraction of the time.

CHAPTER SIX

Dealing with Common Illnesses and Ailments

by Philip Stapleburg BVSc (PRET) MRCVS

Humans have always been fascinated by the power, stealth and beauty of birds of prey, and they have been the source of inspiration for many artists, poets and men of power. But even these majestic rulers of the skies are vulnerable. Life in captivity has its own unique problems and this is often reflected in the diseases to which they are prone. Everyone who owns a raptor has a responsibility to become familiar with the health problems that could threaten a bird's life so that preventative measures can be taken and disease recognised early.

Diseases of the Respiratory Tract

The respiratory system of birds is very different from that of mammals, both anatomically and physiologically. Birds have no diaphragm and their lungs are stuck to the dorsal thoracic wall. These lungs are not as elastic as mammalian lungs, and they lack alveoli. Gas diffusion takes place in this counter-current situation which refers to the mechanism where blood in the blood vessels and in the airways moves in opposite directions, increasing the surface area contact of air to blood, thus greatly increasing the efficacy of gaseous-exchange. When the sternum moves down air flows into the abdominal air sacs, which function as a bellows system, and when the sternum moves up air is forced through the lungs and other air sacs and exhaled. Movement of the sternum must not be restricted with bandages as this will cause the bird to suffocate.

Diseases can affect both the upper and the lower respiratory tracts. Problems sometimes involve one or the other, and sometimes both. The upper respiratory tract comprises the nostrils (nares), head sinuses and laryngeal area. The trachea, syrinx, mainstem bronchi, primary bronchi, parabronchi, lungs and air sacs form the lower respiratory tract.

Diseases of the respiratory system are often encountered in birds of prey, and they can be caused by a variety of infectious agents. It is unlikely that the lay person will be able to distinguish between various causes, but you should be able to recognise the fact that your bird has a respiratory disease early so that the vet can make a specific diagnosis. Respiratory disease should always be regarded as serious.

There are various symptoms to look out for.

Symptoms of upper respiratory disease

- nasal discharge
- soiling of feathers around nare and cere with dried discharge
- head-shaking
- sneezing
- blocking of nostrils with dried discharge
- watery eyes as a result of ocular discharge, and conjunctivitis
- sinusitis, which gives the head a swollen appearance or makes the eyes bulge; this often leads to asymmetry if the head is viewed from the front
- open-mouthed breathing
- inflammatory lesions, with or without discharge inside the mouth or back of throat
- audible clicks and wheezes as air flows through the nasal passage

Symptoms of lower respiratory disease

- weight loss with or without the loss of appetite
- increased respiratory effort
- increased respiratory rate
- tail-bobbing (up and down movement of the tail when the bird is breathing)
- wings held slightly away from the body, sometimes with the neck extended
- depression
- fluffed-up appearance
- audible moist clicking or wheezing sounds when breathing
- open-mouthed breathing
- change in voice
- coughing
- exercise intolerance

The organisms involved are:

- **Viral Infections**. Infections such as Poxvirus infections can cause raised lesions on the unfeathered parts such as the nares and ceres.
- **Bacterial Infections**. Various bacteria may be involved. The most common ones are *Pseudomonas aeruginosa*, *Klebsiella pneumonia*, *Pasteurella multocida* but other bacteria can cause disease in a compromised patient.
- **Fungal Infections**. *Aspergillus fumigatus* is by far the most frequently encountered infection of the respiratory system of

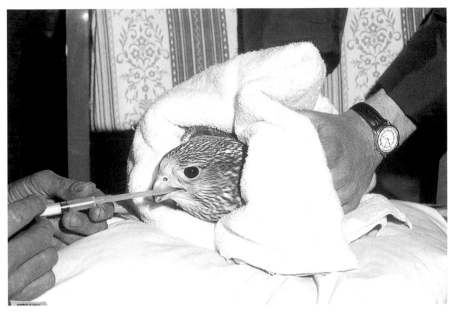

Crop-tubing a sick falcon

raptors. This is a very serious condition and is discussed in more detail below.

- **Mycoplasma** spp.
- **Chlamydia** spp.
- **Parasites**. These include gapeworms (*Syngamus trachea* and *Cyathostoma* spp) and air sac nematodes (*Serratospiculum* spp).

Aspergillosis

Aspergillosis is caused when *Aspergillus fumigatus* spores enter the respiratory tract, which then leads to a fungal growth inside the body. The disease can present itself in different forms but usually develops into fungal granulomas in the air sacs or trachea fungal granulomas refer to the lesions caused by the growth of fungus inside the body. These lesions consist of an accumulation of fungus and inflammatory material. It is very difficult to recognise this disease early and symptoms are usually noticed only when the disease is already in an advanced state. The emphasis in the control of this condition must therefore be on prevention rather than cure.

The most important principles of disease prevention are:

- Prevent exposure to the disease causing agent
- Maintain a healthy, functional immune system
- Use prophylactic medication correctly where indicated
- Vaccinate against the disease where possible.

There is at present no vaccine available for use with raptors, but we will examine the other measures you can take.

Aspergillus fumigatus grows on almost any organic matter and prefers moist, dark places with limited ventilation. Birds should therefore be kept in a dry, well-lit area with good ventilation. Your weathering should not be close to rotting and decaying material such as compost heaps, cut grass, hay or piles of wood. The area where you keep your bird must be clean, with special emphasis on corners, cracks and junctions, as this is where growth of the fungus often starts. It is important to remove faecal matter and debris, and to change absorbent material such as wood shavings regularly.

An important source of *Aspergillus* spores is dirty and mouldy travelling boxes. When birds are transported in contaminated boxes they are exposed to millions of harmful spores, which will almost certainly lead to this disease. Travelling boxes must therefore be kept in a dry place with good ventilation and left open when not in use.

You can improve your bird's immune system with good care and nutrition. Talk to your vet and more experienced falconers. A good, well-balanced diet goes a long way to improving your bird's ability to fight disease. There are very good dietary supplements available that can help to provide essential nutrients, vitamins and minerals.

Stress is a very important prelude to many illnesses, as it lowers the ability of the immune system to fight disease. A certain amount of stress is unavoidable but it should be kept to the bare minimum. Cigarette and other smoke, fumes from aerosol cans and other sources, and even dust, can diminish the effectiveness of the respiratory tract's defence systems, allowing pathogens to enter the body with ease, so avoid these respiratory stressors at all cost.

Certain species of birds are more susceptible to aspergillosis and prophylactic treatment is sometimes needed. If yours is a 'high-risk' bird, ask your vet for advice. Species that are particularly susceptible include:

- gyrfalcons (*Falco rusticollis*)
- golden eagles (*Aquila chrysaetos*)
- goshawks (*Accipiter gentillis*)
- red-tailed hawks (*Buteo jamaicensis*)
- snowy owls (*Nyctea scandiaca*)

The symptoms of aspergillosis are vague at first and often become more pronounced after a period of stress. Birds can be depressed and lose weight, and you may notice vomiting and a drop in food intake. The condition can be diagnosed with the aid of blood tests, radiographs, tracheal swabs for culture and endoscopic examination with a sample collection for fungal culture and histopathology. If diagnosed early, the condition can sometimes be cured with intensive antifungal treatment in hospital. However, many birds contracting this disease will eventually die or be humanely destroyed, usually because the disease is only recognised very late. If the fungal growth is localised, surgical removal may also be curative. The prognosis for hawks with aspergillosis is usually poor but depending on the location of the fungal growth and the stage of the disease, a small number may survive.

Annual check-ups, which could include haematology, blood biochemistry and full-body radiographs are recommended, so that any suspicious indications can be examined. Many birds die of aspergillosis every year, but the number can be substantially lowered if owners follow these principles.

Diseases of the Alimentary Tract

The alimentary tract is divided into the following parts: oral cavity, oesophagus, crop, proventriculus, ventriculus, small intestine, large intestine and cloaca. Infections involving the digestive system can be caused by viruses, bacteria, protozoal organisms, endoparasites and sometimes fungal organisms such as *Candida*. It is beyond the scope of this book to discuss every condition in detail, so I will concentrate on those that you are most likely to encounter.

Birds have the ability to hide their symptoms, making it difficult for the inexperienced person to identify the presence of disease. However, there are a few procedures that will help you spot when something is wrong.

First, weigh your bird regularly, as described on pages 102-4. When birds are ill they will show a downward curve in their daily weight chart, usually before any other symptoms are noticeable. This should alert you to consult your vet.

Secondly, familiarise yourself with the normal appearance, volume and frequency of your bird's faeces. If any abnormalities are present for more than a day, you should seek professional attention. Faecal samples can be examined and tested for certain pathogens. Also monitor the castings carefully, and any deviation from the normal appearance, frequency or consistency should be investigated.

Thirdly, the type and amount of food consumed must also be recorded daily, and changes in water intake noted.

Record-keeping is a very valuable aid to the early diagnosis of disease. You will quickly gain the knowledge and experience you need if you maintain regular records. If you draw a graph of your bird's progress, you will easily be able to recognise problems when the graph shows a deviation.

Trichomoniasis
This is a disease of the oral cavity that sometimes extends into the

crop and respiratory system. It is caused by protozoa and is characterised by white, cheesy lesions inside the mouth. It is a very common condition in pigeons and doves and is transmitted to raptors when they eat these birds as prey. If your bird has eaten pigeon-derived material and white raised nodules appear in the oral cavity, it is likely that it has trichomoniasis. The condition can be confirmed by scraping some of the lesions and examining the material as a wet preparation under the microscope; the organisms can be seen swimming around on the slide.

Treatment is normally easy and effective. Metronidazole or carnidazole can be used, but get advice from your vet. Treating it without proper guidance can put your bird in danger. If cases of trichomoniasis are left untreated the necrotic lesions can interfere with the bird's ability to catch and swallow food and can even destroy the vital structures of the oral cavity itself. But the disease can easily be prevented by not allowing your bird to eat wild pigeon.

Other diseases can cause similar lesions in the oral cavity, so it is important to get your vet to confirm a diagnosis before treatment is given. These diseases include heresvirus stomatitis, poxvirus stomatitis and secondary bacterial and candidial infections.

Raptors with oral infections often indulge in head-flicking and usually have a poor appetite. There are differences in susceptibility between raptor species, and certain *Trichomonas* strains are more virulent than others.

Endoparasites of the Alimentary Tract

Parasites of the gastro-intestinal system commonly lead to a loss of condition. Periods of stress or the presence of disease will cause the effects of parasites which might not otherwise be apparent to become obvious. The different internal parasites, or endoparasites as they are called, can be classified as:

* threadworms
* roundworms
* tapeworms
* flatworms

It is very important to identify the specific parasite before deworming your bird. There is no such thing as an all-round wormer and every parasite will have to be treated specifically.

The clinical signs of parasites are vague unless there are a great many of them. Symptoms can include the following:

* weight loss with or without appetite loss
* head-flicking

- regurgitation
- diarrhoea
- depression

Faecal samples can be examined to look for worm eggs; the vet will do faecal flotations to identify the parasites involved. Faecal examination must be done in conjunction with a physical examination before treatment is given.

You should not allow your bird to eat the entrails of her prey, as they are a potential source of infection.

Bacterial Enteritis

Primary bacterial infections of the gastro-intestinal system are common in raptor chicks but not in adult birds. It usually occurs when there are insufficient normal intestinal flora present, which then allows other pathogenic bacteria to flourish. Bacterial enteritis may also be caused when the intestines of avian prey are eaten. Bacterial organisms such as *Salmonella enteriditis* and *Escherichia coli* are commonly responsible.

Diagnosis is based on bacterial culture and sensitivity testing of the faeces. The normal enteric flora can be replaced by using avian probiotics such as Avipro (Vetark).

The symptoms include anorexia, diarrhoea, regurgitation and foul-smelling faeces. Dehydration and weight loss occurs and eventually the bird will die. Antibiotic treatment combined with rehydration therapy and supportive care is necessary in birds suffering from bacterial enteritis.

Coccidiosis

This is a protozoal disease of mostly juvenile and compromised birds, which is a term used to describe a bird that is injured or in ill health, whatever the reason. *Eimeria* spp are normally the causative organism but *Isospara* spp can also be involved. Diarrhoea, weight loss and a decreased appetite are common symptoms, and diagnosis is based on wet preparation examinations of the faeces. Antibiotic treatment with sulphonamides is usually successful.

Candidiasis

This organism is an opportunist that rarely causes primary disease, but is commonly present as a secondary pathogen in a sick or immuno-compromised bird, or a bird that has been treated with antibiotics. A normal, healthy individual's immune system is usually sufficient to control this single-cell fungus. Competition from normal enteric flora will also inhibit candida growth. It is only when these controlling factors are suppressed that the yeast cells are able to multiply and cause an active infection. Stress is also an important factor. Treatment usually involves removing the primary cause, re-establishing the normal gastro-intestinal flora and treating the candidiasis with Nystatin. Some strains of candida are resistant to Nystatin, however, and alternative antifungal medications should be used.

The organisms can be seen on faecal smears that are stained with Diff Quick or Gram stain. A few non-budding yeasts are regarded as normal but budding organisms indicate an active infection.

Conditions of the Limbs

Bumblefoot
Apart from traumatic injuries of the wings and legs, which frequently occur, and should always receive immediate veterinary attention, the only other common limb condition is bumblefoot. This is a common and potentially fatal condition that affects the weight-bearing surfaces of the feet. During the early stages it can be recognised as a reddened thinning of the skin which can have a shiny appearance with or without the presence of wounds. The dermal papillae will become smooth and the surrounding skin inflamed. Bacteria will eventually enter the area and the resulting infection is capable of damaging and destroying vital structures such as the flexor tendons, joints and bones. The lesions are painful and warm to the touch. Septicaemia may develop in some cases and this can result in death.

There are various stages and degrees of bumblefoot. Cases that are diagnosed early respond well to treatment whereas longstanding and neglected cases are more difficult to treat successfully, and may damage the feet permanently.

There are many causes, but sustained pressure on the ventral surfaces of the feet seems to be the most common. This is brought about by factors such as hard, unyielding perches (e.g. hardwood, metal or concrete), a heavy, overweight bird or injuries to one limb which result in the other having to carry the bird's whole weight. Repeated uncontrolled bating can also damage the feet, and this in turn can lead to the development of bumblefoot.

If there is excessive pressure on the sole for a long enough period, it will eventually affect the flow of blood to the tissue. This poor blood supply will then cause cellular damage. Because of this damage the superficial layers of the skin separate from the underlying tissues and the skin becomes more permeable. It is at this stage that bacteria enter the area to complicate matters and add to the damage. *Staphylococcus aureus* is the bacterium most frequently isolated but other bacteria such as *E. coli* and *Pseudomonas* as well as fungal organisms can also be involved.

Other, less common causes of bumblefoot are wounds to the feet such as puncture wounds caused by talons and bite wounds from prey such as squirrels. Internal disease can also predispose birds to bumblefoot.

Falcons are more likely to develop bumblefoot than any other raptor, but whatever species you have, you should take preventative measures. Most cases of bumblefoot can be prevented by ensuring that the bird does not get overweight (although this is not possible during the moult – see page 115) and that the bird is not allowed to bate repeatedly. It is very important to weigh and exercise your bird regularly, and to keep accurate notes of how much food is given, how much is consumed, the type of food fed and daily body weights. Perches must be padded or wrapped with material such as Astroturf to reduce the incidence of pressure damage to the feet. A balanced diet with mineral and vitamin supplements is also important. You should examine your bird's feet regularly and have them checked annually or even six-monthly by a vet. Any lesion or injury to the feet should be seen by a vet.

Severe cases of bumblefoot need aggressive treatment. Surgical drainage and debridement, which is the surgical removal of dead and damaged tissue, is sometimes necessary and may have to be repeated more than once. Swabs or bacterial culture should always be taken and sensitivity testing done so that the appropriate antibiotic treatment can be given. Wounds need to be flushed and cleaned regularly and pus and necrotic tissue must be removed daily. Topical disinfectants such as povidone-iodine or chlorhexidine can be used to flush wounds.

Protective dressings are necessary to keep lesions free from recontamination. After surgery the affected foot will be bandaged – the degree of damage and the areas affected will determine the method of bandaging used. Toes can be bandaged with the wound site left open, which will take pressure off the damaged part of the sole. Ball bandages are also frequently used. Dressings must be changed regularly. Topical treatments must always be used in combination with a systemic antibiotic medication based on the results of bacterial culture and sensitivity testing.

Sadly some cases of bumblefoot are neglected for too long and do not respond well to treatment, but proper preventative measures and immediate veterinary attention to problem areas will be successful in most cases.

Other Conditions

Avian Tuberculosis
This disease is caused by *Mycobacterium* spp and it can manifest itself in various ways. *Mycobacterium avium* is most frequently involved. It

can affect any organ, but the symptoms can go undetected until very late in the course of the disease. The most common clinical sign is weight loss despite a good appetite, which once again underlines the importance of weighing your bird daily. Although it is less common than many other conditions, it is still extremely important to be aware of it, as it can be dangerous.

Avian tuberculosis is extremely contagious, and carriers of the disease can contaminate the environment when shedding the organism. The contaminated area can remain unsafe for a very long time and it can be extremely difficult to make it safe.

It could be called a silent killer. You should only buy your bird from a reputable breeder, and imported birds should be thoroughly examined. An examination ought to include full faecal inspection, blood biochemistry and haematology and full-body X–rays. Suspected cases can be endoscopically examined for internal lesions. Biopsies are helpful to confirm a diagnosis.

Once the disease is diagnosed the prognosis is poor. Treatment is very expensive and often not successful. Birds that are treated will have to be kept in strict quarantine and should be regarded as a major health hazard. I recommend euthanasia if it is confirmed in your bird.

Tuberculosis is a zoonotic disease, which means that people can also be infected by the organism. There is a particular danger to people with weak immune systems such as AIDS sufferers, and special care should be taken in these cases.

Raptor Herpes Viruses
There are many different herpes viruses. Almost every mammal and bird species can be infected by them, and owls and birds of prey are no exception. Herpes virus infections are usually fatal in birds of prey. Some birds are probably carriers of the disease and although they might not show any signs themselves, they might shed the infectious agent. This needs to be investigated and researched to determine its importance, especially in view of the fact that certain prey birds could also be carriers of herpes viruses. Infected birds usually die after a few days of depression and anorexia.

Falcon herpes virus usually only infects longwings, although owls can also be susceptible. Owl herpes virus is more frequently involved in infections of owls.

Owls will often show small white lesions on the oropharyngeal mucosal surfaces which are mucous membranes of the mouth and throat area especially on the palate.

There are other diseases that have similar macroscopic lesions, so it is important that the cause of death is investigated, especially where other birds might have been in contact with the affected bird. Contact with wild raptors should be avoided and newly acquired birds must always be placed in quarantine for approximately 40 days.

There is no effective treatment as yet, so prevention is the only option.

Lead Poisoning

This condition is caused when lead is ingested, usually accidentally, when a bird has been fed quarry which has not had the shot completely removed. It is almost impossible to remove every piece of lead shot from a rabbit or pigeon, and I therefore recommend that you do not take the risk of feeding your bird shot game.

Symptoms of lead poisoning include lethargy, regurgitation, gastro-intestinal stasis, green stools, weakness and neurological signs. Some birds will sit on their hocks 'holding hands' – a symptom only seen with lead poisoning. The diagnosis can be confirmed with X–rays, which reveal lead in the gastro-intestinal tract. Treatment is usually supportive. Calcium edta and D–Penicillamine should be used to bind the lead and make it harmless. This is very important if the bird's life is to be saved. If the bird has fits, they must be controlled with anti-convulsive medications. Birds with lead poisoning will need intensive veterinary care and the sooner the treatment starts the better the chance of survival.

Lead poisoning will only result from the ingestion of lead and not from lead lodged somewhere in the body as a result of being shot. The body will encapsulate such a foreign body and the lead will not be absorbed systemically. Pieces of lead are sometimes seen on X–rays of wild raptors, but they are usually left alone.

First-Aid in the Field

It is wise to prepare yourself for any problems that might arise in the field. Most people will take special care to avoid accidents, but they often happen when they are least expected. You must have the knowledge and dexterity to administer first-aid in the field. At the very least you should discuss the basics of first-aid with your vet, but a proper veterinary first-aid course would be even better.

When you are in the field the nearest veterinary hospital may be hours away and a good knowledge of first-aid can save your bird's life. Carry a well-equipped first-aid kit which is practical, easy to carry and easy to use at all times. The following items should be included:

- **A syringe and feeding tube**. This will be used to crop-dose a bird with fluids, electrolytes etc. The bird should be cast by one person whilst another passes the tube over the base of the tongue and into the crop. The head must be secured with the less frequently used hand and care must be taken not to introduce the tube into the tracheal opening at the base of the tongue. The equipment must be kept clean and disinfected after it has been used.

- **A small blanket, towel or space blanket**. This can be used to restrain a bird or to wrap around it when it is wet, to prevent hypothermia. A blanket must never be wrapped too tightly around the body as this will interfere with normal breathing movements. When a bird of prey has been drenched by cold water the wind-chill factor must also be taken into account. A blanket will help protect against the wind until you can reach the nearest building or vehicle. If possible, it is advisable to hood the bird to limit stress in these situations.

- **A pair of tweezers**. Tweezers can be used to remove foreign bodies and dirt from wounds before disinfecting them. They can also be used to remove food which may be stuck in the crop or back of throat.

- **Small artery forceps**. If an artery or vein has been severed, a life-threatening haemorrhage is possible. If you see a pulsating artery, use these forceps to gently pinch off the bleeding end, and twist it round until the bleeding stops.

- **A packet of 4/0 sterile catgut**. If pinching with forceps does not stop bleeding from an artery, catgut can be used to tie off the vessel. Your vet can supply it and also show you how to tie off a blood vessel.

- **A silver nitrate pencil**. This is a chemical way to stop bleeding, but it must only be used on bleeding talons and beak tips. Take care not to touch the skin or sensitive parts with the pencil because it is irritating to other tissues. Slightly moisten the tip of the pencil before using it on a bleeding nail, then apply even pressure for a few seconds on the bleeding area.

- **A few swabs, a little cotton-wool and a handful of cotton-tipped earbuds**. These items will help to clean and cover small wounds. You can also use swabs and cotton-wool to apply pressure to bleeding wounds. Pressure is important in stopping bleeding.

- **Disinfecting solution such as povidone-iodine or chlorhexidine**. Wounds that occur in the field are always contaminated, and must be thoroughly cleaned before disinfectants are used. Deep or more serious wounds will also need antibiotic treatment, but you should not try this without the supervision of your vet. Cotton-tipped applicators or swabs can be used to apply disinfectants, and a small syringe will also come in handy to draw up and apply the disinfecting solution.

- **Bandaging material such as Vetrap and Micropore**. When a raptor injures one of its limbs in the field it is important to immobilise it to prevent further injury until it can be taken to a vet. Wings should be bandaged up in a normal closed position.

A figure-of-eight bandage is easy to apply and you should familiarise yourself with the various bandaging techniques.

- **A flexible finger splint**. When a leg is fractured, you should use a splint to immobilise it, padding it with cotton-wool first. The splint can then be fixed in position with a bandage. Remember that this is only an emergency measure and you should seek proper treatment as soon as possible.
- **Electrolyte mixture**. A ready-made solution such as Ringers Lactate or Hartmann's Solution can be used. There are also powdered formulae such as Lectade available which can be dissolved in clean water. These fluids can be administered in cases of shock and injury. The fluid should be drawn up in a syringe and kept close to your own body for approximately five minutes to warm it to body temperature. Give the bird 2 per cent of its body weight every two hours.
- **Glucose powder and fresh water**. Certain falcons and sparrowhawks may develop hypoglycaemia if they are flown too light. They will appear weak and exhausted. Hypoglycaemia is life-threatening and must be treated immediately. Dissolve the powder in a small amount of fresh water before administering it via a crop tube. Some falconers prefer to carry a jar of honey with them but glucose-saline or dissolved glucose powder is more effective. Hypoglycaemia will cause fits and death if it is left untreated.

The most important first-aid principles to remember are:

- treat the bird for shock and stop any bleeding
- limit stress
- provide heat
- immobilise fractured legs and wings to prevent further damage and pain
- clean and disinfect wounds
- seek veterinary help as soon as possible.

The Development of Avian Veterinary Medicine and Surgery

The quality of avian veterinary science is constantly improving as many committed professionals apply their knowledge and experience to caring for sick and injured birds. During the second half of this century there have been major advances in both medicine and surgery, and diagnostic techniques are becoming more and more refined. Treatments continue to improve and increase the success rate in treating sick birds.

New drugs are being developed and patients benefit increasingly from newer, safer and more effective treatment. A good example is the progress that has been made in the development of new-generation antibiotics, which offer a wider spectrum of effectiveness against bacterial infections. Generally the drugs available today are far superior to those of 20 years ago. This pattern will undoubtedly continue into the next century. Great progress has also been made in the administration of safe anaesthetics and the development of Isoflurane has revolutionised general anaesthesia in exotic species. This is currently regarded as the gold standard in avian anaesthesia.

More conditions and infectious agents are being identified and more and more veterinarians, biologists, virologists, microbiologists and pathologists are becoming involved in the study of avian diseases. Their findings are published regularly and information is exchanged on the Internet.

But the continued development and refinement of this discipline rely on committed individuals who strive to make this world a happier and healthier place for birds to live in. It is not only the professionals in the medical field that make this possible, but also the many people who own, train and care for these amazing animals. We must never lose sight of the fact that we are the caretakers of the earth, and we must ensure that other species have a future. Our responsibility does not stop with the birds we own, but extends to the millions that fight to survive in the wild every day.

Veterinary Fees

Many people underestimate the expense of veterinary care, and this can lead to birds being deprived of the attention they need. When people buy a bird, they may hope that she will never fall ill or be injured, but unfortunately this is not always the case. You should therefore be well aware, right from the outset, of the level of veterinary fees that could be incurred. Fees will vary from surgery to surgery but veterinary care of a high standard is usually expensive, and as the standard of veterinary medicine improves, it will only become more so. Veterinary care must not be taken lightly; to do so could have tragic consequences for your bird. So ask your vet for a price list and discuss the cost of annual check-ups and ancillary tests.

You will be very much mistaken if you believe that the PDSA will treat your sick bird. Although they will initiate treatment in an emergency, they will then refer you to a private surgery. Certain diseases and injuries can cost hundreds of pounds to treat, and I strongly recommend you insure your bird for veterinary expenses.

Health-monitoring visits and preventative care are far cheaper than the treatment of severe diseases, so the importance of primary health care cannot be overemphasised.

CHAPTER SEVEN

The Attributes, Etiquette and Rules of Falconry

Commitment

For me, falconry is the ultimate working partnership between man and animal. If I were asked to explain its appeal, I would simply say 'Challenge'. Each day the falconer is challenging his abilities in the pursuit of excellence. One constantly strives to condition one's hawk until she reaches her peak of physical fitness and she is able to take

A Bengal eagle-owl on a creance

quarry showing tactical aptitude. Only then can you take pleasure from all your hard work and dedication, for you and your bird will be pursuing the sport of falconry to the full.

As I have said, one of the most vital attributes that any falconer must possess – and this is something that can never be taught – is patience. The patience to sit and understand one's hawk is probably the most important characteristic separating good falconers from bad ones. Buying a bird of prey is as easy as buying a kitten, but a bird of prey can live for 25 years or more, and requires the same commitment for the whole of that time.

You will form a bond with your bird which you may like to think is more than merely food-orientated. Unfortunately it is not. Unlike a dog, a hawk is not loyal, and if it is flown out of condition it will simply accelerate into the distance. A colleague once told me a sad story concerning a Harris hawk, a bird he had flown intensively for many years. She was a solid hunter with all the right attributes. She was steady and bold, and knew her job. She worked exceedingly well over dogs and ferrets, but above all, she was trustworthy – or so he thought. For six years she had been flown by the same person, and throughout this period neither went astray nor gave cause for alarm. One crisp morning however, whilst out hawking over familiar land, the bird began to bate fiercely. Unable to see any quarry, my colleague allowed her to take to the wing, knowing that her eyesight was far superior to his. He expected her to drop onto a rabbit, but was overcome by an overwhelming feeling of emptiness when she just flew on and on and on, not even pausing for one last look at her partner and keeper for the last half-dozen years.

Why this should have occurred is a mystery. Her hunting weight was right, the scales were unquestionably correct and she was in a fine state of health, so what went wrong? Falconry leaves us with many unanswered questions. Perhaps the only answer is that a bird of prey is born wild and despite being intensively manned and trained will revert back very quickly. If there is a moral to this story, it is that the loyalty between man and hawk is purely one-sided. They will never love and respect us as we do them, and will only tolerate us if they are sufficiently hungry.

It is impossible to understand fully the thinking of a raptor. I do not believe that there is anyone who can be classed as an expert in this field. From the day our sporting career begins until it is over, we are continuously learning. Birds of prey are unpredictable, impulsive and certainly opportunistic, and it is this that keeps us on tenterhooks whenever a hawk is released from the fist.

Dedication is the key to the sport for it is dedication that will keep us both learning and progressing. No doubt there will be times when you wonder whether you were cut out for falconry. You may have a season when everything goes wrong. This is the time when total dedication is required. Those with the strength of character to keep plugging away when things become tough will be far better, stronger and knowledgeable falconers in the end. And if one has a genuine passion, one will find rewards every day.

Respecting the Sport

A falconer should feel a great sense of pride whenever his bird makes a kill. Managing of a hawk from eyass to fully-trained hunter is hard, tedious work, often requiring extra time and effort as the hunting season approaches.

Unfortunately, there are falconers who take the training of their birds casually, supplying endless bagged quarry which has no sporting chance of escape, only to find that they are put to shame in the hunting season by hawks that have been prepared throughout professionally. Although the use of bagged quarry is acceptable in many countries, in Great Britain it is strictly illegal. Those who do not train their birds to an acceptable standard, and who may resort to such measures, are going totally against modern-day rules and regulations.

People who ask their birds to make continuous kills are similarly to be condemned. Although quality hawking will produce exciting flights and result in many kills, a bird should never be asked to kill just for the sake of adding another statistic to one's bag at the end of the season. A couple of kills which have been the result of quality flights, should provide a more pleasing day than sheer quantity. For me, this is true falconry – a well-trained, fit, energetic bird being flown at quarry which is just as fit and which has a fifty-fifty chance of escape.

There are many individuals and organisations that favour the banning of field sports. Under current legislation, we are free to pursue the sport we love, and provided we obey the law and conduct ourselves in a professional way, we can show that we are behaving responsibly. But it only takes a few 'cowboys' to bring the sport into disrepute, which could lead to a ban on our activities. We have a duty to abide by the rules, such as those relating to the taking of game only in season, and those who do not are simply giving ammunition to the sport's opponents.

The question is often asked, how the future of falconry can be safeguarded? I believe the answer is simple. Beginners must receive continual help and guidance from those who have greater experience. Within time, this generation will be in a position to help others in exactly the same way. But those who believe they can advise others after only six months or so can jeopardise this process, as the next cohort of falconers will start off with bad advice. I strongly recommend that every falconer, of whatever standard, should be a member of one of the large organisations, such as the British Falconers' Club or the British Hawking Association. At the very least, you should be a member of a well-established local club. As a member you will receive information on developments in key areas such as the law. Beginners who are taught and advised properly are the lifeline of the sport.

Falconry is not cruel, although there may be individual undesirables who treat their birds badly. Nor does it involve killing for its own sake. Birds that hunt do so to provide food for the falconer. Nothing that a bird of mine kills is in vain. It either provides food for me and my friends, or it is frozen to supply meals for my birds all year round. The sport will flourish if the highest standards of bird management are maintained by all, and if the rules and traditions are respected.

A falcon enjoying her bath.

CHAPTER EIGHT

The Law

by PC Paul Beecroft

There have been many changes which have affected falconry over the past 50 years. Since the Protection of Birds Act 1954, the trapping of wild birds has been illegal, and this led to a decline in falconry; there were fewer birds available and it became much harder to obtain a wild bird legally to pursue the sport.

The past 20 years, however, have seen an incredible increase in the number of birds now available for falconry purposes. The captive breeding of many species is now quite common and growing every year. Species that were rarely seen in Great Britain, such as the Harris hawk, red-tailed buzzard, saker falcon and lanner falcon, were imported and as a result many of these birds, and others, now breed readily in captivity. This, as a consequence, meant the number of birds of prey in captivity has grown steadily.

Falconry in Great Britain does not require a licence, and anyone can own or keep a bird of prey. In certain cases, some species will need a registration document, but this is not to be confused with a licence.

NOTE: It is vital that falconers are aware of up-to-date changes in the law. You may wish to visit the DEFRA website www.helpline@defra.gsi.gov.uk on a regular basis.

The Wildlife and Countryside Act (WLCA) 1981

This Act came into force in September 1982, and included provisions relating to all hawks and falcons that were being kept in captivity. All hawks and falcons were included in Schedule 4 of the Act, and the Act required that all of these birds be registered with the Department of the Environment (DoE) as it was then known, DEFRA as it is now. Each bird had its own uniquely numbered ring, and a registration document was issued, similar to a vehicle registration document.

There are three categories of bird in captivity:

- The main group comprises those that have been bred in captivity. These birds are fitted with a closed, metal ring, and the majority can be bought and sold quite freely, subject to certain conditions.
- The second group comprises wild disabled birds which cannot be returned to the wild. These birds cannot be sold under any circumstances and are fitted with cable-tie identification rings.

- The final group are those birds that had either been taken from the wild under licence (which is no longer permitted) or birds that are imported under licence. These birds are also fitted with a cable-tie identification ring.

There are certain cases when captive-bred birds of prey can be fitted with cable-tie rings. This normally occurs when the breeder leaves it too late to fit a closed metal ring, or when it has fallen off because it was fitted onto the bird too early.

During the next ten years, the number of birds of prey being kept in captivity increased, and by 1992, approximately 16,000 specimens were registered with the DEFRA. Eight species made up 81 per cent of all birds registered:

Kestrel	3,855	Sparrowhawk	1,157
Common buzzard	2,472	Red-tailed buzzard	1,062
Harris hawk	1,815	Goshawk	880
Peregrine falcon	1,418	Merlin	361

Also during 1992, 6,100 initial registrations and 4,750 transfers were recorded. The Government decided that the time had come to substantially reduce the number of birds on the Schedule 4 list. Wild populations of many species had dramatically increased since 1981, in particular the kestrel, common buzzard and sparrowhawk. Also, as non-native birds were not free-living in Britain, and therefore could not be taken from the wild, a substantial number of these species could also be removed from the requirements of the Act. By doing this, resources could be used to strengthen protection for the less common species that were to remain on Schedule 4.

In May 1994, therefore, Schedule 4 was amended, and the following birds of prey are the only ones now subject to ringing and registration under Section 7 WLCA 1981.

Common Name	Scientific Name
Buzzard, honey	*Pernis apivorus*
Eagle, adalbert's	*Aquila adalbert*
Eagle, golden	*Aquila chrysaetos*
Eagle, great Philippine	*Pithecophaga jefferyi*
Eagle, imperial	*Aquila heliaca*
Eagle, New Guinea	*Harpyopsis novaeguineae*
Eagle, white-tailed	*Haliaeetus albicilla*
Falcon, barbary	*Falco pelegrinoides*
Falcon, gyr	*Falco rusticolus*
Falcon, peregrine	*Falco peregrinus*
Fish eagle, Madagascar	*Haliaeetus vociferoides*

Forest falcon, Plumbeous	*Micrastur plumbeus*
Goshawk	*Accipiter gentilis*
Harrier, hen	*Circus cyaneus*
Harrier, marsh	*Circus aeruginosus*
Harrier, Montagu's	*Circus pygargus*
Hawk, Galapagos	*Buteo galapagoensis*
Hawk, grey-backed	*Leucopternis occidentalis*
Hawk, Hawaiian	*Buteo solitarius*
Hawk, Ridgway's	*Buteo ridgwayi*
Hawk, white-necked	*Leucopternis lacernulata*
Hawk-eagle, Wallace's	*Spizaetus lacernulata*
Hobby	*Falco subbuteo*
Honey-buzzard, black	*Henicopernis infuscata*
Kestrel, lesser	*Falco naumanni*
Kestrel, Mauritius	*Falco punctatus*
Kite, red	*Milvus milvus*
Merlin	*Falco columbarius*
Osprey	*Pandion haliuetus*
Sea eagle, Palla's	*Haliaeetus leucortphus*
Sea eagle, Steller's	*Haliaeetus pelagicus*
Serpent eagle, Andaman	*Spilornis elgini*
Serpent eagle, Madagascar	*Eutriochis astur*
Serpent eagle, mountain	*Spilornis kinabaluensis*
Sparrowhawk, New Britain	*Accipiter brachyurus*
Sparrowhawk, Gundlach's	*Accipiter gundlachii*
Sparrowhawk, imitator	*Accipiter imitator*
Sparrowhawk, small	*Accipiter nanus*

NB
All of the above species are also included in Schedule 1 WLCA 1981 and are therefore protected by a special penalty.

Some of the raptors now listed in Schedule 4 will not be readily found in captivity in Great Britain, whilst others will not be found at all.

Registration Documents
Registration documents are issued to the keepers who hold Schedule 4 birds – i.e. those that are subject to ringing and registration under Section 7. The document gives a number of details, including the date of expiry (registration must be renewed every three years) and the name and address of the keeper, together with his or her identification number, issued by DEFRA. It will also include a number of details about the bird, including species, gender, ring number and the date the keeper acquired the bird. It may also

include the date the bird was hatched if it was born in captivity, and the parents' ring numbers. The origin of the bird is also included (this will normally be 'captive bred', 'wild disabled' or 'imported'). There are times however when it may read 'not known'. This occurs when the history of the bird is in doubt, e.g. a bird that has recently been 'found' with falconry equipment attached but it is not ringed or one that has been seized at some point by the police and again its true origin is in question. There are also transfer details if the bird is passed on or sold, and conditions relating to its sale. The document clearly states that registration does not legalise taking or possession, and the fact the bird has been registered does not mean that it was legally obtained and therefore legally held.

Section 7(1) of the Act says:

If any person
keeps/has in his possession – or under his control –
any bird included in Schedule 4
which has not been
registered and ringed or marked
in accordance with the regulations made
by the Secretary of State,
he shall be guilty of an offence
and liable to a special penalty.

Hybrids

A hybrid bird is the result of the crossbreeding of two or more species, and hybrids are now quite common in captivity. They are required to be ringed and registered if one of the parent birds or any lineal ancestor is included in Schedule 4. A peregrine x gyr falcon or a peregrine x saker, for example, would be a registerable species, but a lanner x saker would not as both species are excluded from Schedule 4.

Wild Birds in Captivity

A wild bird is defined as any bird of a kind which is a resident in, or is a visitor to, Great Britain in a wild state. For the purposes of birds of prey, this includes all the indigenous species listed in Schedule 4, and also the buzzard, kestrel and sparrowhawk. There are other species of raptor that are known to visit Great Britain, however, such as the red-footed falcon, so if in doubt always check with the proper authorities.

Section 1(2)(a) of the Act states:

If any person has in his
possession or control

any
live or dead
wild bird
or any part of, or anything derived from,
such a bird
he shall be guilty of an offence.

There are certain exceptions to this but the onus of proof lies with the person who has the bird in his possession to show that he has the bird legally. The prosecution only needs to show that the person was in possession or control of the bird.

Other Registration Offences
Section 17 WLCA 1981 states:

If any person makes a
statement or representation
or furnishes a
document or information
which he knows to be false in a
material particular
he shall be guilty of an offence.

And further:

If any person
recklessly makes a
statement or representation
or furnishes a
document or information
which is false in a material particular
he shall be guilty of an offence.

Following a conviction for any of the above offences, Section 7(3)(a) will take effect. This says:

If any person
keeps
or
has in his possession or under his control
any bird included in Schedule 4
within five years of having been convicted of an
offence under this part for which a special
penalty is provided
he shall be guilty of an offence.

Following conviction in respect of any bird that is included in Schedule 1 is a special penalty offence. All hawks and falcons included in Schedule 1 are also included in Schedule 4. This means that a person subject of a conviction is liable to a fine of up to £5,000 but in any event a person will automatically be subject of Section 7 (3)(a). This means for a period of five years he/she is not permitted to own, keep or have in their possession any species of bird that is included in Schedule 4. Section 7 (3)(a) will not take effect, however, if a conditional discharge was given for the original offence.

Sale of Wild Birds
It is an offence to sell any wild bird, or to offer one for sale, or to publish an advertisement which implies that you buy or sell them.

Non-Schedule 4 Birds
The law on ringing and registration does not apply to a bird that is not included on Schedule 4. Such birds include the Harris hawk, the red-tailed buzzard, the lanner falcon, and also the common buzzard, the sparrowhawk and the kestrel, which are indigenous. It is not an offence to keep a non-Schedule 4 bird that is not ringed but it is an offence to sell or display one. (The legislation covering this is explained below.) It is, however, considered irresponsible to keep a bird that is not fitted with some type of ring whether closed or split. In the case of the common buzzard, sparrowhawk and kestrel, the onus of proof will always be with the keeper or owner to prove that the bird is captive-bred and not wild. A ring fitted to the bird does not legitimatise it but it does in many cases assist in tracing it back to its origin.

There are certain regulations that are specific to barn owls, which are worth mentioning. In its wild state, the barn owl has suffered a considerable decline in numbers due to shooting, poisoning and loss of habitat. In captivity, however, these birds are prolific breeders, with three and even four clutches a year being recorded. This has led to a huge number of surplus barn owls being offered for sale in magazines and newspapers.

It is reported that there could be three or four times as many birds in captivity than there are in the wild. Owing to the reduced numbers in the wild, many of those bred in captivity have been released into the wild. Some of these release schemes have been done with great thought and care; unfortunately, however, some have not, which has resulted in many released captive-bred birds starving to death or ending up in rescue centres, having been unable to fend for themselves. As a result of this, the barn owl has now been included in Part 1 of Schedule 9 WLCA 1981, and Section 14(b) of the Act now applies.

This states:

If any person
releases or allows to escape
into the wild any animal which
is included in Part 1 of Schedule 9
he shall be guilty of an offence.

Captive-bred barn owls can, however, still be released, as long as a licence, obtainable from DEFRA, has been issued. Wild barn owls taken into care can be released back to the wild under a general licence.

The sale of a captive-bred barn owl is also controlled. It must be fitted with a closed ring issued by the British Bird Council or the International Ornithological Association. It is therefore illegal to sell a barn owl with only a breeder's ring fitted.

CITES

In 1975, the Convention on International Trade in Endangered Species of Wild Fauna and Flora (CITES) came into force. Its aims were to regulate the international trade in specimens of animals, birds and plants, including derivatives. Over 130 countries are now party to the Convention, which is administered at an international level by a secretariat based in Switzerland. Conferences take place every two to three years and lists of species subject to protection are reviewed. Each party to the convention has designated a management authority. In the UK, this is DEFRA on the mainland and the Department of Agriculture in Northern Ireland.

The animals, birds and plants subject to CITES controls are listed in three appendices. Appendix I includes those species which are threatened with extinction. Any species included in this appendix cannot be traded, except in exceptional circumstances. Under certain conditions such as for scientific or zoological purposes, individual exemption may be granted, but they must be licensed by the management authorities of both importing and exporting countries. There are also exemptions for captive-bred specimens. The birds of prey and owls listed in this appendix are:

- Spanish imperial eagle
- imperial eagle
- white-tailed sea eagle
- American bald eagle
- harpy eagle
- Philippine eagle
- Seychelles kestrel

- Aldabra kestrel
- Mauritius kestrel
- peregrine falcon
- Barbary falcon
- lugger falcon
- gyrfalcon
- Cuban hook-billed kite
- Andean condor
- Californian condor
- Madagascar owl
- forest spotted owl
- giant scops
- Norfolk Island boobook
- Christmas Island owl

Appendix II lists species which are not immediately threatened with extinction, but which may become so if trade is not controlled. It also contains so-called look-alike species which are controlled because of their similarity in appearance to the other regulated species. Commercial trade in these species is permitted under CITES when the country of origin has issued an export permit. Appendix II includes all birds of prey and owls not included in Appendix I. There are no birds of prey included in Appendix III

The Control of Trade in Endangered Species (Enforcement) Regulations 1997
CITES is implemented in the European Union by European Council (EC) regulations, which are directly applicable in national law. On 1 June 1997, EC Regulation 338/97 came into force. It changed the regulations concerning the sale, purchase and display for commercial purposes of many birds of prey. All species, including owls, are included in one way or another in this new regulation.

Under this regulation, fauna and flora have been divided into four annexes. Only Annexes A and B are relevant to birds of prey; as only the king vulture is included in Annex C, and none in Annex D.

The following species are listed in Annex A.

- Andean condor
- Californian condor
- osprey
- cinerous vulture
- Egyptian vulture
- Eurasian griffon
- lammergeier
- Adalbert's eagle
- Bonnelli's eagle
- booted eagle
- golden eagle
- greater spotted eagle

- harpy eagle
- imperial eagle
- lesser spotted eagle
- Madagascar serpent eagle
- Philippine eagle
- sea eagles
- short-toed snake eagle
- black kite
- black-winged kite
- Cuban hook-billed kite
- red kite
- Montagu's harrier
- northern harrier
- pallid harrier
- west marsh harrier
- Eurasian sparrowhawk
- goshawk
- grey-back hawk
- Levant sparrowhawk
- common buzzard
- European honey-buzzard
- long-legged buzzard
- rough-legged buzzard
- Barbary falcon
- common kestrel
- Eleonora's falcon
- Eurasian hobby
- gyrfalcon
- lagger falcon
- lanner falcon
- lesser kestrel
- Mauritius kestrel
- merlin
- Newton's kestrel
- peregrine falcon
- red-footed falcon
- saker falcon
- Seychelles kestrel
- barn owl
- boreal owl
- Christmas hawk-owl
- Eurasian eagle-owl
- Eurasian pygmy owl
- Eurasian scops owl
- forest owlet
- great grey owl
- lesser eagle-owl
- little owl
- long-eared owl
- Norfolk Island boobook
- northern hawk-owl
- short-eared owl
- snowy owl
- Sokoke scops owl
- Soumagne's owl
- tawny owl
- Ural owl

From this it can be seen that all indigenous falcons, hawks and owls are included in this annex.

Sales Controls Relating to Annex A

The purchase, sale and display for commercial purposes of Annex A birds of prey or their hybrids is prohibited unless a certificate has been issued by DEFRA or other EU management authority. Article 10 certificates, or sales certificates as they are being referred to, will only be valid for one sale unless the bird originates from a 'recognised breeder', in which case it is valid for all subsequent sales as long as the certificate travels with the bird.

The following regulations apply to recognised breeders:

- They must keep accurate records and make them available for inspection.

- They do not require a certificate to advertise specimens for sale prior to the eggs being laid.
- Certificates permitting sale can be issued by DEFRA semi-completed, and can then be completed by the breeder when the chicks are hatched.

All live Annex A birds must be marked before any sale. This applies to both recognised breeders and individuals. Captive-bred birds must be fitted with a close ring of the correct size for the species. If this is not possible for one reason or another, then a microchip must be inserted into the bird. A tattoo, cable-tie or any other marking is not acceptable. Birds which have been taken wild or whose origin is unknown must be microchipped. The ring number or microchip number/code must be recorded on any permit or sales certificate.

If an Annex A bird is also included in Schedule 4 WLCA 1981, it will still need to be ringed and registered in accordance with the requirements of that Act. This means that the species must be registered to the seller and the registration document must also accompany the bird. The tear-off slip at the bottom should also be completed and returned to DEFRA with details of the purchaser. If the bird is cable-tied, it will also have to be microchipped prior to any sale, and an individual sales exemption obtained.

Article 10 certificates are also required to sell dead Annex A birds which were captive-bred or lawfully taken from the wild within the EU. Sellers must keep accurate records and submit annual reports to DEFRA. Any certificate issued is valid for one sale only. You will also need a certificate if you want to sell any part or derivative of a bird listed in Annex A, including eggs, semen, blood or feathers.

If any Annex A bird, whether alive or dead, or any part or derivative of such a bird is to be displayed to the public for a commercial purpose, then an Article 10 certificate must be obtained. This would include falconry displays at country shows, corporate hunting days, falconry courses and film work. Even if the event is for a recognised charity, a certificate is still required. Falconry centres need an individual certificate for every bird that is being displayed to the public.

An Article 10 certificate will be required if you want to purchase an Annex A species when the seller does not have his own certificate. This situation does not often arise – indeed, it will probably only happen when the specimen is illegal in the first place. Do not be tempted to buy such a bird either to avoid paperwork or because it is cheap. The penalty is severe – up to two years' imprisonment.

Import/Export Controls
For the purposes of import and export from 1 June 1997, species will fall into one of three categories:

- **Annex A**: Specially protected species, which may only be imported or exported for non-commercial purposes, unless they are captive-bred in accordance with certain criteria.
- **Annex B**: Species not included in Annex A but which member states have agreed that importation should be restricted on conservation grounds. (Applications to import specimens of these species for non-commercial purposes will be considered on their merits, in the same way as for Annex A specimens. There are many restricted species that are subject of an import suspension. The list is subject to change and all enquiries for a current list should be directed to the CITES enquiry desk at DEFRA.
- **Annex B (cont)**: All other diurnal and nocturnal birds of prey (except Annex C below)
- **Annex C**: Only one species of bird is included on this annex, namely the king vulture (*sarcoramphus papa*). A self-completed imported notification form must be presented to customs when importing this species. An export permit or certificate of origin will also be required from the exporting country. A permit will also be needed to (re)export it from the community.

Movement of CITES Specimens within the EU

CITES specimens may be freely circulated within the EU, although evidence may be required to confirm that they were imported or acquired lawfully. There are however a number of conditions:

- An Article 10 certificate is required before Annex A specimens can be sold.
- If the import certificate specified the location at which a live bird of prey is to be kept, such as a wild-taken bird, then a certificate will be required before it can be moved from that location. Captive-bred birds can normally be moved freely under the holder's copy of the original import permit.
- In the case of split consignments, the permittee's copy may be exchanged for the required number of certificates confirming that the specimens were imported in accordance with the regulations.
- DEFRA, or other relevant EU management authority, may also issue certificates confirming that the birds concerned were imported or acquired lawfully.

Certificates can only be issued for the purposes laid down in the regulations and member states cannot require the issue of certificates for any other purpose.

Application forms to obtain Article 10 certificates are available by writing to DEFRA, whose address can be found in the Appendix or by contacting the CITES website – www.cites.org

Enforcement
In the UK the penalties for violation of CITES are provided for in the Control of Trade in Endangered Species (Enforcement) Regulations 1997 (COTES). Enforcement is a shared responsibility between HM Customs and Excise, who are responsible for import offences, and the police, who are responsible for sales controls.

Next to habitat destruction, the illegal trade in endangered species offers the greatest threat to the world's rarest animals, birds and plants. It is believed that after drugs, the trade in endangered species is the second largest criminal activity in the world, with an annual turnover estimated at $5 billion.

Liaison between Customs and Excise, the police, DEFRA and others is now commonplace and the UK features prominently in prosecuting offenders against CITES and COTES regulations. Most UK police forces now have wildlife liaison officers, whose job is to investigate offences against wildlife crime in general and to deal with COTES offences in particular. It is anticipated that over the forthcoming years these types of offences will be more rigorously enforced. Falconers and keepers should take special care not to bring falconry into disrepute by breaking the law. Each conviction brings media attention and does a lot of harm, especially when wild-taken birds are involved. Stay within the law and help keep falconry safe.

The following is a list of possible offences against COTES. If you have any doubts about any part of the legislation then you should check with the authorities before you act.

Article 10 sales certificates offences

- making a false statement or representation
- furnishing a document or information which is false in any particular material
- using or furnishing a false, falsified, or an invalid permit or certificate or one altered without authorisation for any purpose in connection with the EC regulations

Sales offences

- selling a bird without an Article 10 certificate
- selling a bird that is not ringed or marked in accordance with the regulations
- keeping a bird for sale, offering for sale and transporting a bird for sale without an Article 10 certificate

- exchanging a bird for another or for any other item without an Article 10 certificate
- hiring or bartering for a bird without an Article 10 certificate

Purchase offences

- purchasing a bird for which an Article 10 certificate has not been issued
- purchasing a bird that has not been ringed or marked in accordance with the regulations
- offering to purchase either of the above

Display offences

- displaying birds to the public for commercial gain without an Article 10 certificate for each bird displayed, including falconry demonstrations and static displays at country shows and game fairs – this includes money put into a donation box
- taking part in hunting days, falconry courses, corporate days etc without an Article 10 certificate for each bird used
- using a bird in filming, advertisements, still photographs etc for commercial gain without an Article 10 certificate.

This list is by no means complete and is only intended as a basic guide to the most common pitfalls.

Penalties for COTES offences
The new regulations on COTES offences provide for stricter penalties for offenders. A magistrate's court now has the power to order imprisonment for up to three months, together with fines up to £5,000, while in the crown court, the sentence may be up to two years' imprisonment and an unlimited monetary fine.

You should also remember that you could be both imprisoned and fined. Also note that each offence can be dealt with individually, so if you sold two common buzzards that did not have Article 10 certificates, the maximum fine in a magistrate's court would be £10,000. Moreover, the court will order the forfeiture of the bird and it may order the forfeiture of any other item that was used to commit the offence, such as a motor vehicle.

Finally, there are a number of new powers that have been given to both the police and DEFRA wildlife inspectorate. This is mainly the power to enter and inspect premises under certain conditions and to take blood or tissue samples to determine ancestry or identity. A new offence has been created of impersonating a wildlife inspector, as there have been reports of people pretending to be wildlife inspectors to gain entry to premises where collections of birds are kept.

DoE Rings

As I have said, there are two types of ring found on birds of prey, the closed-metal ring and the plastic cable-tie. All rings issued by DEFRA are easily recognised. In the case of closed rings, they normally have four or five numbers followed by some letters printed sideways on and then a letter denoting the ring size. The DEFRA cable-tie rings come in a number of colours, but the ring number always starts with the letters 'UK' followed by five numbers. A clear, plastic sleeving generally covers the ring number, and after a period of time, it can often be difficult to read the number when dirt etc. gets between the sleeving and the ring.

Cable-tie rings are open to abuse. They can be taken off one bird and put onto another. A cable-tie ring and registration document can be worth up to £200, depending on the species it was originally issued to. It is always worthwhile checking the registration document for the age of the bird and comparing it with the bird the ring is fitted to. A number of people have been caught this way, but it may take an expert to discover the deception.

Breeders' Rings

These rings are obtainable from several sources and are advertised in a number of magazines. They come in a variety of colours and the breeder can choose what he wants stamped on the ring. In the main, breeders use numbers followed by their initials, the ring size and the year. So a ring might read something like 001 PKB 96W. Breeders should not fit rings they have left over from previous years onto a current year's offspring, but I am sure that this will occur from time to time, leading to unnecessary confusion.

Game Laws

All those that practise the sport of falconry must have a good knowledge off, and totally abide by legislation that concerns quarry.

Although Game species are protected during their breeding season, there are open seasons throughout the year when they can be hunted. The following table shows these times.

For further information concerning Game laws, one should contact DEFRA and ask for a copy of the Wildlife and Countryside Act 1981.

Type of Game	Start of season	End of season
Pheasant*	1 October	1 February
Partridge*	1 September	1 February
Grouse*	12 August	10 December
Blackgame*	20 August	10 December
Ptarmigan*	12 August	10 December
Capercaillie	1 October	31 January
Common Snipe*	12 August	31 January
Woodcock* *England & Wales*	1 October	31 January
Woodcock* *Scotland*	1 September	31 January
Duck & Goose (*inland*)	1 September	31 January
Duck & Goose (*Foreshore above high water mark of ordinary spring tides*)	1 September	20 February
Coot & Moorhen	1 September	31 January
Golden Plover	1 September	31 January
Curlew	1 September	31 January
Hare*	No close season	

*Species marked with an * require a game licence available from the Post Office which is renewable annually*

Conclusion:
Is Falconry for You?

For every hawk which is flown and entered regularly, ten or twenty are not. They are the ones which are often bought by people who have given hawk ownership little or no thought. They can offer their bird no more than a meaningless life of seclusion in a wooden-panelled weathering. They often keep them as status symbols, as pets or for financial gain, and have little or no respect for falconry and its traditions. Although these keepers call themselves falconers, they do very little to help the image and respectability of the sport.

Not everyone who is genuinely interested in falconry is in a position to do justice to their birds. In fact, very few people will not have to make changes in their lives to accommodate a sport which makes such high demands. Those who think that they can, despite circumstances being against them, all too soon allow their standards to drop. Although this book will hopefully have given you an insight into the time, expense and skill involved in owning a bird of prey, some of you may still be tempted to start just because a friend has told you you can. All I can say is, does your friend pursue falconry in a manner which reflects the true spirit of the sport? I would strongly recommend you to seek professional advice or attend a course before you make up your mind.

Having said that, I hope I have been able to help and encourage those of you who do have the right commitment and lifestyle to take the next step and attend a falconry course. If pursued in the right way, falconry will give you endless pleasure and many happy memories. Your bird will live with the dignity and self-respect she deserves, you will meet and become friends with others who have the same love of the sport and its traditions, whilst occasionally, you will enjoy the company of birds you can only dream of actually owning. As a member of a club, you may have the chance to visit some breathtaking countryside and to fly over some of the best land on offer.

Finally, if you apply thought and dedication to every decision you make, I am sure your sporting career will be long and successful. I wish you the very best of luck and happy hawking.

A peregrine feeding from the fist

Appendix
Useful Addresses

Falconry Suppliers

Mr Jim Moss
Crown Falconry
48 Kent Street
Hasland
Derbyshire
Tel: 01246 237213

Eagle-Owl Falconry
c/o Lee William Harris
E-mail:
leewilliamharris@hotmail.com

Telemetry

Luksander telemetry system
c/o Mr Tony Scott
Northumberland Bird of Prey
Centre
Peter Barratts Garden Centre
Newcastle Upon Tyne
NE3 5EN

Lamping Equipment

Clulite Engineering Ltd
Unit 6
Bedford Road
Petersfield
Hampshire
GU32 3ULJ
Tel: 01730 264672
Fax: 01730 260475

Falconry Courses

**The Eagle-Owl School of
Falconry (London)**
c/o Lee William Harris
E-mail:
leewilliamharris@hotmail.com

Falconry and Owl Centres

**The New Forest Owl
Sanctuary**
Crow Lane
Ringwood
Hampshire
BH24 3EA
Tel: 01425 476487

Registration and Licensing

DEFRA
www.helpline@defra.gsi.gov.uk
Tel: 0845 933 5577

Independent Bird Register
Tiercel House
Falcon Close
Scotton
North Yorks
DL9 3RB
Tel: 0870 608 8500

Microchip Companies

Pettrac Identichip
AVID PLC
Holroyd Suite
Oak Hall
Sheffield Park
Uckfield
East Sussex
TN22 3QY
Tel: 01825 791096
Fax: 01825 791006

Animal Care Ltd
Common Road
Dunnington
York
YO1 5RU
Tel: 01904 488661
Fax: 01904 488184

RS Biotech
Brook Street
Alva
Clackmannanshire
Scotland
FK12 5JJ
Tel: 01259 760335
Fax: 01259 762824

Falconry Clubs

The Welsh Hawking Club
www.thewelshhawkingclub.com

British Falconers' Club
www.britishfalconersclub.co.uk

British Hawking Association
www.thebha.co.uk

Other Addresses

**Bird of Prey Centre –
Management & Consultancy**
c/o Lee William Harris
E-mail:
leewilliamharris@hotmail.com

Countryside Alliance
367 Kennington Rd
London
SE11 4PT
Tel: 0171 582 5432

Cage & Aviary Birds
IPC Magazines
Kings Reach Towers
Stamford Street
London
SE1
Tel: 0870 444 5000

The Falconer's Magazine
Arrowsmith Court
Station Approach
Broadstone
Dorset
BH18 8PN
Tel: 0870 224 7820

Index

Spaniel relaxing with falcons.